KV-388-065

Hamlyn

Freshwater Fishes

A CONCISE GUIDE IN COLOUR

Freshwater Fishes

by J. Vostradovský

Illustrated by J. Malý

Hamlyn

London New York Sydney Toronto

Translated by D. Coxon

Designed and produced by Artia for
THE HAMLYN PUBLISHING GROUP LIMITED
London New York Sydney Toronto
Astronaut House, Feltham, Middlesex

© Copyright Artia 1973

Reprinted 1974

All Rights Reserved. No part of this publication may be
reproduced or transmitted in any form or by any means,
electronic or mechanical, including photocopy, recording,
or any information storage and retrieval system, without
permission in writing from the copyright owner.

ISBN 0 600 33476 7

Printed in Czechoslovakia

Contents

Introduction 9

Water Environment 11
  An Insight into Hydrobiology 11
  Water Temperature 16
  Light in Water 18
  The Fish and Sound 20
  Echolocation 22

The Anatomy of Fishes 24
  The Skeleton 24
  The Muscles 25
  The Blood, the Heart and the Gills 26
  The Digestive Organs 27
  The Air-bladder 29
  The Reproductive Organs 30
  The Nervous System 31
  The Lateral Line 31
  Sight 32
  Hearing 33
  Smell and Taste 33
  The Skin 34

The Scales, the Growth and the Age of Fishes 36
  The Scales 36

The Number of Scales in the Lateral Line 38
The Growth of Fishes 40
The Age of Fishes 43

Fishes and the Water Environment 45
The Shape of the Fish's Body 45
The Shape of the Head and the Caudal Fin 48
The Changing Colours of Fishes 50
Different Living Conditions and the Needs of Fishes 53
Migration and the Change in the Location of Fishes 55

Fishes and Food 58
When Fishes Eat 58
The Food of Small Fishes 60
The Food of Non-predatory Fishes 60
The Food of Predatory Fishes 62
The Pike—the Most Common Predatory Fish 64
The Fishes and the Algae in the Water 66
The Smell of Mud 67
The Effect of Algal Blooms 68
Artificial Bait 69
Plates 71

Index of Common Names 249

Index of Latin Names 251

INTRODUCTION

The pace of life today calls for some form of active relaxation. It is often sought in the countryside, in rambling or in water sports for instance; and those who once try their hand at fishing fall for its charm for ever. What brings greater satisfaction and diversion at the same time than time spent near the ever changing face of water and in an exciting struggle with a fish? Nature generously gives away its treasures to those who understand it. Fishermen want to know as much as possible about nature in order to preserve it and also to take pleasure in it through relaxation. They are not satisfied any more with knowledge acceptable to their fathers and friends; they increasingly want to know more about fish biology, the water environment and to keep abreast with the advance in fishing techniques. They want to master everything that will help them to appreciate more the chain of events and the phenomena they meet in fishing and which contribute to the satisfaction of their passion for fishing.

It would be a mistake to believe that one becomes a good fisherman by mere study of angling literature. It is only a guide which explains in theory some phenomena, perhaps unclear at first sight. Only many years of residence by lakes and rivers, combined with a passion for nature, gives an understanding of the apparently mysterious under-water life and teaches an enjoyment of the real pleasures of fishing.

Of course there are many manuals for fishermen. Some of them are almost recipe books and expect the reader to hold the rod in one hand and the respective instructions in the other, while others praise both the fishermen and the water environment in lyrical undertones. The aim of this book is modest: it is to give the reader, above all the beginner, a digest of information about fishes living in European waters, with some interesting facts about their biology and a selection of approved techniques in catching even the most cunning fishes. Undoubtedly anglers who have already spent many quiet hours at the riverside will find in it some confirmation of and perhaps even an addition to their own experiences.

Water Environment

An Insight into Hydrobiology

It is common knowledge that roughly two thirds of the earth's surface is covered by water. The biggest part of this, approximately 132,000,000 square miles, is occupied by the oceans and seas, including salt lakes, whereas the fresh waters, such as rivers, lakes, ponds and reservoirs take up only about 1,000,000 square miles. The waters of the earth's surface represent a vast and immensely varied habitat for the huge number of water organisms: man is most interested in those which can be used for food or can be used in other ways.

This book is predominantly concerned with life in the fresh waters of rivers and reservoirs, and being intended for fishermen, will concentrate primarily on fishes. At the same time it must be remembered that fishes are not the only inhabitants of water, but only one of the highest forms of life in that habitat. To understand the conditions of life in water and so be successful conservationists and anglers it is necessary to analyse the fundamental preconditions of life in water, in fact to obtain an insight into hydrobiology.

Hydrobiology is the science which deals with the living conditions of water plants and animals and their interrelationship. It draws on the disciplines of biology, chemistry, physics, biochemistry, biophysics, hydrology and geology: the scientist who works in hydrobiology must have a wide knowledge and an ability to make correct deductions and to see the connection between the varied types of fundamental living conditions. On many occasions he must have the courage to depart from the traditional methods and the accepted theories, but then he must be able to prove and defend his views. In hydrobiology there is always something new being discovered, especially about the general equilibrium of life in water.

The living conditions in water are generally similar to those on land: the sun's radiation as a source of heat and light, the oxygen necessary for breathing, the nutriment important for the structure and growth of organisms, a suitable environment, and water, of course, without which life is impossible. Water itself, which on land is a clearly defined item, is here in surplus and provides the living environment itself. That is why its quality is so important, especially its cleanliness which is becoming one of the most pressing problems of our time.

Water is an especially distinctive environment, owing to its chemical and physical characteristics. In nature chemically pure water with a neutral reaction does not exist. Water in nature always contains a smaller or a larger amount of dissolved minerals, which determine its hardness and influence its reactions. It also contains liquefied gases, such as oxygen and carbon dioxide, and also important organic substances. The thermal characteristics of water are significant when compared to those of minerals and air. It provides an environment with a stable temperature. Water achieves its highest density at 4°C and not at freezing point, which is a further decisive factor for life in water. Similarly the changes in volume and energy during the transformation of water into ice and vice versa are important. The density and viscosity of water likewise influence the form of water organisms and the arrangement of their organs. Some characteristics of water will be dealt with in detail in the individual chapters, but first the general aspects of life in water must be examined.

In water and generally in nature, life is an association of organisms, from the smallest to the largest, both plant and animal. It is well known that this combination is not always peaceful and idyllic; but we are more concerned with life cycles and continuous organic changes. In the natural process growth follows birth, death follows life. The dead bodies of plants and animals and their excrement are decomposed by bacteria and partly by fungi and moulds, and the complex organic substances are gradually reduced to their simple mineral constituents, such as water, carbon dioxide and other gases, and salts. These are all the basic foundation stones of a new generation of flora and, through their mediation, also of animals. Algae and plants in general are the first builders because of their ability to carry out photosynthesis, the conversion of carbon dioxide, water and inorganic salts into complex organic compounds in the presence of sunlight and chlorophyll.

In water the leading part is played by plankton, a collection of small plant and animal organisms passively floating. The phytoplankton, the plant part of the plankton, is largely formed by algae, which are the primary producers. The zooplankton, the animal part of the plankton, consists of tiny animals which are just visible to the human eye. Of those in warm waters the most numerous are small crustaceans with refractive eye-lenses, called *Daphnia*. The animals of the zooplankton consume algae and also eat one another according to the natural law of the stronger eating the weaker. Animals living on the bottom or clinging to the plants there continue this activity. They are the larvae of amphibious insects, such as the Mayfly, Caddis Fly, Stonefly and others. In ponds and still water, they are the larvae of gnats which often make a network of miniature corridors on the bed which they inhabit. The bottom-living animals are either predatory, eating animals of the zooplankton, or they live on the dead algae and vegetable remnants which sink to the bottom. These animals are an important, sometimes a decisive, part of the food of those fishes which usually feed at the bottom, such as the Carp, the Bream and the Ruffe, and they play an important part in the diet of the Grayling, the Trout and others.

Small fishes are an important transitional type of food. They are an important consumer of plankton. Later on they themselves become the object of predatory fishes, which in effect use them as an intermediary to obtain nutriment otherwise inaccessible. These facts indicate the possibility of increasing the productivity of water by raising the amount of nutriment in it, that is by fertilization. Modern production of fishes in ponds involves this and results in a greater output of fishes per acre than ever before. Fertilization of rivers is taken care of by human settlement, the organic waste of which is unpleasantly profuse, and also by some industrial plants. In so far as the river manages to cope with the inflow of organic matter and break it down by self-purification, it can be incredibly full of fishes as its water is so rich in nutriment. But the taste of fishes from such waters is affected. Catastrophy can ensue from a weak river flow with a high water temperature; in such conditions normal purification is insufficient and fishes begin to die.

In a general survey of water life the enemies of fishes must also be considered. They include bacteria, moulds, and such fish parasites as fish leeches and larger crustaceans such as the Carp Louse. The most destructive are predatory water insects and their larvae. They not only eat the plankton and the bottom-living organisms and in this way reduce fish food, but they also attack the fry which they can sometimes destroy completely. It is surprising how many enemies of fishes are found in water which has not been properly looked after. Three to five million individuals, weighing about 550 lbs were found in only 2.5 acres of a particularly rich reservoir, an amount which represents a considerable legion of fish enemies. Such creatures are killed by chemicals, or they can be caught by means of various light devices, etc. This is when hydrobiology comes into its own as it supplies data for such operations, especially in ponds and reservoirs.

From this brief glance at hydrobiology, it is evident that it is not simply a pure science but that it has practical applications.

Now it is essential to consider further fundamental factors which crucially affect water life and other phenomena which can be met with while fishing.

Water Temperature

Both air and land get warm and become cold several times more quickly than water. Seas, large lakes and sizeable reservoirs notably influence and moderate the climate of their environment. They reduce the differences in temperature by making the surrounding air cooler in summer and warmer in winter. It is noticeable that even smaller reservoirs influence the temperature of their immediate environment.

Water becomes warmer from the direct effect of the sun's radiation, which penetrates only to a certain depth. The warmth spreads to greater depths by conduction but here it is obviously less intense. Water can also become warmer through contact with banks or the air. Water currents and the wind, ruffling the upper surface of the water, are also important factors. Still waters are warmest at the surface in summer and the reverse is true in winter. The process of warming and cooling of the water in large lakes and reservoirs is obviously longer than in ponds or even streams. The water of deeper and larger reservoirs keeps warm until late autumn, so that the Carp feed as late as the end of November, sometimes in the beginning of December, when the nearby ponds and rivers are usually frozen and the fishes have become torpid. The reverse is true in spring when the shallow waters of ponds and rivers become warmer more easily and the fishes become more active sooner.

Water temperature is an important factor for life in water. The blood temperature of fishes and other water organisms fluctuates and is dependent on the temperature of the water. The lower the temperature, the slower is the process of living. This characteristic is especially true in the case of warmth-loving fishes, such as the Carp, the Catfish, the Barbel and others; if they are located in waters which are too cold they grow slowly and do not spawn. Cold-loving fishes, such as the Trout, on the contrary, cannot tolerate excessively warm water, in which they lack oxygen. Similarly they do not thrive in water which is too cold: they multiply but grow slowly and do not reach their usual weight, as all the digested food is spent in the production of energy (which is greater in quickly flowing water). It is possible to indicate the optimal temperature range for each fish, for example that for the Trout lies between 10 and 15 °C, that for the Pike between 15 and 20°C and that for the Carp between 22 and 25°C.

Water temperature also influences the amount of oxygen which dissolves in it. A matter for consideration is whether the water has achieved the maximum possible absorption of oxygen at a particular temperature, as a considerable amount of oxygen in highly organically polluted water is consumed during biochemical decomposition. A great deficiency of oxygen is found in the lower water layers of reservoirs and lakes and sometimes it is non-existent during warm seasons. It goes without saying that it is pointless to expect fishes to feed at depths where oxygen is lacking and that a knowledge of the laws of hydrobiology is important.

In any given water, the temperature also affects the spawning process. Carp require a water temperature of at least 18°C, Catfish are even more particular and Grayling are satisfied with a water temperature of 8°C.

Subsequently the fertilized spawn develops more quickly in warmer water.

Light in Water

The main source of light filtering through the water is the sun and at night the moon and the stars. The sun's radiation is of fundamental importance for water life as it supplies the necessary energy for photosynthesis; the sun's radiation does not penetrate to a great depth, as can be seen by the fact that phytoplankton is stratified only to a depth of several metres, while zooplankton only achieves a greater depth by movement.

Light is very important for fishes to direct their search for food. Experience confirms that the fishes evidently perceive even the slightest amount of light. A comparison of the intensity of the three sources of the light mentioned above best illustrates this. The intensity of the sun's radiation on cloudless summer days can exceed 1,000,000 luxes (units of illumination). In comparison the full moon shines through the darkness of the night at an intensity of a mere 0.2 lux. During a clear starlit night without moonlight it is only 0.0003 lux and even then some fishes can be expected to feed, such as the Pikeperch, Catfish and Carp, not to mention the Burbot and Eel. Given such conditions, consideration must be given to ways other than sight by which fishes find food, such as by smell and touch.

The illumination of water during the daytime fluctuates considerably and is dependent on the height of the sun above the horizon and on the shade cast by clouds. Not all the sun's rays falling on the water surface penetrate and illuminate it. This only happens if the sun's rays descend at an angle of 90°, namely at right angles to the surface. Such a situation only arises in the tropics and then for only a limited period. In fact the lower the sun sinks towards the horizon, the more light is reflected by the water surface. When the sun's rays fall at an angle of about 20° or below, only a small quantity of light penetrates the water. This means that below the surface of lakes, reservoirs and rivers night falls much earlier than on land and accordingly the angler has to choose a suitable time to start his night's fishing. He should definitely start before dusk when he can easily see what is happening on the surface and has a chance to find out where, how, and on what the fishes are feeding, at that time. At the same time he can choose the most suitable spot and generally discover the situation. This is not only true about catching Carp or Pikeperch, but also applies to fly catching in the evening and at night.

The intensity of the light, which has penetrated the water surface, quickly decreases as the depth becomes greater and as it is dispersed by particles in suspension and by plankton. After the light has passed through a 50m layer of water, its intensity has on average been reduced to a tenth. This reduction is noticeable at dusk, when the depths quickly fade into darkness. At this time the plankton rises to the surface, especially the animal fraction, which is closely followed by small fishes and later predatory fishes, a fact to be considered when fishing in lakes and reservoirs at night. A natural screen is sometimes formed on the surface by ice, which retains between eighty and ninety per cent of the light. But if the ice becomes covered by a mere several centimetres of snow, complete darkness sets in beneath the water surface.

The pellucidity of water has now to be examined. In the majority of fresh waters it is not very good, despite good illumination. The bed of shallow Trout streams can be dimly seen, but only with suitable illumination. Even then all fishes are not visible, especially those resting on the bottom, as they blend into their environment. In lowland rivers and ponds the water is only slightly pellucid. Visibility is also unfavourably influenced by water mist, which is caused by the reflection of light rays from the bottom and by the dispersion of light by the small particles in the water. In autumn, when the number of organisms floating in the water decreases and when the flow of the river is sluggish, it is possible to see to a depth two or three times greater than that possible in summer.

Anglers sometimes incorrectly bemoan the large fish that got away as they do not realize that they were under the influence of an optical illusion. All objects in water appear to be closer and seem to be about one third larger than they really are.

The Fish and Sound

Water is sometimes called a silent world and it is commonly concluded that fishes are dumb. However, research has shown that fishes in their watery habitat produce sounds which, unless amplified, cannot be heard by the human ear. Only a few tropical fishes give sounds which it is possible to hear at some distance.

Fishes produce audible sounds of various origins but they do so only in an emergency. The Carp and the Barbel do so if kept a long time in the air while the hook is being taken out, while the Weatherfish and the Spined Loach produce a special hissing sound when gripped hard.

In the east and the south-east of Europe a special sound device called the 'splasher' is used in catching Catfish. The apparatus has a sabre-shaped handle, 30 to 40 cm long, to which is attached a bowl, 5 to 6 cm in diameter; usually it is carved from a single piece of elm or apple wood. The 'splasher', held gently in the same way as a violin bow, with its bowl under water is pulled backwards and then sharply yanked out of the water. The air, trapped inside the submerged bowl, escapes, making a noise reminiscent of the splashing of small fishes and frogs which entices the Catfish to the surface in the evening. Another explanation claims that the 'splasher' resembles the sounds produced by Catfish hunting in the water. One way or another, it is an effective instrument for fishing.

Lures producing sounds are also well known and consist of rotating strips of metal into which slots have been cut, through which the water flows and produces a sound undetectable to the human ear. These lures are certain to be effective when other baits fail. When fishing for Perch in winter, tiny lures, made from a lead weight and a hook, come in handy. Their effectiveness is explained by the fact that their jerky movements produce sounds similar to those of small Perch and Ruffe when taking food.

If fishing for Perch under ice, it helps to knock rhythmically on a wooden board with a mallet. These sounds attract Perch to the hole cut in the ice, for as yet inexplicable reasons.

Echolocation

Ultrasonic probes are successfully employed in fishing at sea to locate shoals of fishes, to examine the sea bed and determine suitable places for fishing.

A signal transmitted from an ultrasonic probe is reflected by fishes, other objects, or the sea bed and is recorded either on the screen of the receiving apparatus or on a strip of special paper. Very sensitive receivers detect shoals and even individual larger fishes. In passing it must be remembered that fishes sometimes move very quickly and contact can be easily lost.

Less complicated devices, lacking facilities for automatic registration, are better suited to establishing depth rather than finding fishes, as they distinguish with difficulty fishes from other objects, especially near the bottom.

Ultrasonic probes have no special importance in angling, particularly in shallow and small stretches of water. In time they will presumably be useful in larger lakes and reservoirs for which small pocket devices will have to be constructed. Progress can be made in using these probes to establish depth instead of the commonly used plumb-line.

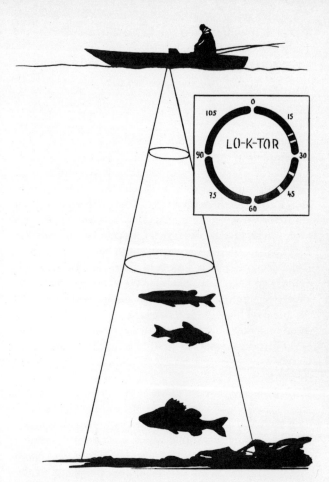

1.. *Ultrasonic waves transmitted from a machine in a boat to the bottom of the lake help in the location of individual larger fishes. (For example, an American sports locator.)*

The Anatomy of Fishes

The word *fish* in this book is used to describe a bony
fish, that is a true vertebrate, the skeleton of which is
always more or less bony. There are drawings and
descriptions of the freshwater and migratory representatives of this group in the illustrated part of the text.
They are animals of various species and shapes, which
spend all their lives in water. Characteristic of such
life is the adhesion of gill filaments to the gill arches,
the growth of gill-covers, scales and the air-bladder.
Fertilization is usually external and the eggs are minute
and numerous. This group of fishes has been devel-
oping over the last 200,000,000 years, whilst their
ancestors came into existence much earlier, about
400,000,000 years ago. Such fishes form over fifty per
cent of current living vertebrates and the total number
of their species amounts to about 20,000 types.

The Skeleton

The skeleton is the main support of the fish's body.
The skeleton of primitive fishes, such as Sturgeons, is
cartilaginous; the skeleton of more highly developed
fishes is formed by an axial support, consisting of the
spine, ribs, intermuscular bones and by an appendage,
to which the muscles of the fins are attached (sometimes called the fin skeleton).

The length of the fish spine varies. It is composed of forty to eighty vertebrae and some long fishes, such as Eels, can have up to 200 vertebrae. The important bones of the skull are the flat opercular bones, by which the age and the growth of the fish can be determined, especially that of the Carp, Perch, Tench and Pike. The important internal bone of the skull is the dermal bone, which characterizes the Salmon family. The visceral arches of the skull include the biting jaws, the hyoid arch and the branchial arches. When eating freshwater fishes (especially of the Carp family), the long thin rib bones prove very unpleasant, as do the y-shaped intermuscular bones, called membrane bones, found for instance in the back muscles of Roach and also in predatory fishes, such as Pike. That is why many species of freshwater fishes form a less than popular dish, although their flesh can be quite tasty. It has been found that the number of Carp intermuscular bones varies and experiments in crossbreeding fishes with the smallest number of membrane bones have been carried out. The results will not be obtainable for several years.

Finally, the remaining part of the fish's skeletal framework is represented by the fin skeleton.

The Muscles

The fish's skeleton is covered by muscular tissue, the same as that of the higher vertebrates and which consists of two types of muscles. The muscles formed by the lateral bands of tissue are the muscles of motion, the second type are the smooth muscles of the internal organs. Separate groups of muscles can be found also in the head, trunk and fins. Well developed for instance are the jaw muscles of predatory fishes or the pharyngeal teeth muscles of the Carp family. The great lateral muscles, used for swimming, are along the sides of the body. The trunk muscles are formed by a series of segments, corresponding in number to the scales, in vertical lines. The fin muscles enable them to twist and turn alternately. Lastly the most well-developed muscles of the fish are the spinal muscles.

The Blood, the Heart, and the Gills

Blood plays an important role in the sustenance of life in any given vertebrate. In proportion to body weight, the volume of fish blood is considerably smaller than that of land organisms and, in addition, freshwater fishes have more blood than sea-water species. The more active fishes have more blood than less active fishes, for example the members of the Salmon family have more blood than the Carp. Blood amounts to about one fiftieth of the total body weight. Its most important component is the oval, red cells, containing the blood pigment, haemoglobin, which absorbs oxygen. Blood circulates in the fish body, pumped round by contractions of the heart which consists of a single auricle and ventricle. From the size of the heart, it is possible to estimate the mobility of the fish. The heart of freshwater fishes and those perpetually mobile is always larger than the heart of sea fishes and fishes that rest on the bottom. It follows that the size of the heart is always related to the fish's way of life.

Blood is carried from the heart to the main breathing organ of the fish, namely the gills, where it receives its charge of oxygen. The gills are located at the side of the head behind four gill arches, covered by the opercular bones. The front part of the gill arches is covered by the gill filaments, the number of which is sometimes an important characteristic feature. The gill folds are on the opposite side. They contain branched capillaries responsible for the transference of gases in the water. Their total surface represents a vast area. Apart from gills, fishes can breathe through subsidiary organs, such as the skin, the gut and the skin of the oral cavity. Some types of fish such as Carp in an emergency can breathe on the surface by swallowing gulps of air. For Carp this is not normal, but indicative of deteriorating living conditions.

The fishes most sensitive to the oxygen content of water are the members of the Salmon family. The Carp family are less sensitive, and indeed the Crucian Carp is very resistant to a lack of oxygen. This is a consideration when transporting small fishes to be used as a bait for predatory fishes. A small amount of water in the bait can is advisable as this becomes agitated and the oxygen content increases.

The Digestive Organs

The digestive system begins with the oral opening and cavity, from which the food is carried to the pharynx,

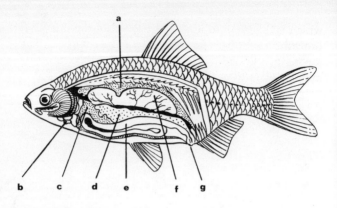

2. The anatomy of internal organs

a) kidneys, b) heart, c) liver, d) reproductive organs, e) intestine, f) air-bladder, g) anus

then to the oesophagus and the stomach. After the stomach come the small and large intestines and the rectum. The digestive process does not start in the mouth. The teeth of predatory fishes change from time to time and their only function is to hold the prey. Non-predatory fishes, such as the members of the Carp family, have pairs of pharyngeal teeth which are used to crush large pieces of food. The gastric glands lead into the folds of the stomach's mucous membranes and they secrete juices which break down the food and facilitate digestion. The gall tract opens into the small intestine. When the fish is hungry, the content of the gall-bladder is large, when the fish is full, it is usually smaller. The stomach in non-predatory fishes may be absent, in which case food is digested in the intestine, which is longer than usual. The speed of the digestive process is dependent on the water temperature and on the nature of food eaten, but this problem will be mentioned in the chapter dealing with food.

The Air-bladder

The air-bladder is a very important organ in bony fishes. It helps the fish to alternate depth by changing the gas volume of the bladder, which results in a change of the specific weight of the fish.

The shape and the size of the air-bladder varies: it can take the form of only one chamber in the shape of a long tube (for example in members of the Salmon family), or can be divided into two parts (for example in members of the Carp family). The air-bladder starts to develop at an early stage as a flap of the digestive tube. In some fishes the tract connecting the air-bladder with the oesophagus disappears at the adult stage (for example in the Perch). These fishes change the pressure in the air-bladder and its volume by means of a special gas gland, rich in capillaries which receive and transmit gases with the blood. The connection of the air-bladder with the digestive tube is retained in some fishes, as throughout the entire life of members of the Salmon family. Fishes come to the surface for the air necessary to fill the air-bladder initially, after they have used up the yolk-sac and when they start catching their food.

The Reproductive Organs

The reproductive organs are all important for the preservation of the species. European freshwater fishes are, apart from a few exceptions, sexually differentiated and during the breeding season they often move to spawning grounds. The females shed their spawn in the water and it is then fertilized by the sperm of the males. The number of eggs of individual species and different sizes of fishes varies considerably. The most fertile are those species which freely discharge the reproductive cells into the water, such as Burbot, after that follow fishes which lay their eggs on water plants, such as Carp. Less fertile fishes usually guard their spawn (for example the Three-spined Stickleback). The size of the reproductive organs increases as the spawning season approaches and sometimes it can assume as much as a quarter of the total weight of the fish's body. The hatching process depends on the physical condition of the fish and on the water temperature.

Fishes can be divided into three groups according to the season when spawning takes place; firstly there are the fishes breeding in spring (for example Carp, Perch and Catfish families), secondly the autumn breeders, which include the majority of the Salmon family, and finally the winter breeders, such as the Burbot of the Cod family.

The Nervous System

The nervous system is of basic importance in the life of fishes. It may be subdivided into the central organs (the brain and the spinal cord) and the peripheral nervous system (the nerves and nerve ganglions). The shape and the size of the brain of different species of fishes varies considerably. However, in all species it is only one thousandth of the total weight. Its individual parts are the centres of the senses. The cerebellum is largest, whilst the optic lobes and the hind brain lie above it. The olfactory lobes, which are the centre of the sense of smell, project outwards from the brain. Finally the spinal cord, in comparison with the brain, is relatively large and of varied length.

The Lateral Line

Life in water has of necessity created an important sensory organ in fishes, the lateral line, which is not found in land organisms. It is formed by a skin corridor running along the sides of the body, connected to the exterior by short vertical tracts which penetrate the scales. These tracts, filled with mucus, can be noticed on the scales and the sense cells open into them. That is why some fishes can, even if blind, find food. The lateral line of all fish species does not develop in the same way. For example the lateral line of the Bitterling is very short; sometimes the length is increased by a curve (for example *Pelecus cultratus*) or it can be extended to the head (for example the Pike).

Sight

The structure of the fish's eye is similar to the eye of the land vertebrate. However, the cornea is flatter and the lens is ball-shaped. The outer part of the eye is formed by the sclera merging into the cornea at the front. The eye is nourished by a vein deriving blood from the capillaries. In some fishes this vein is supplemented by a layer causing the eyes to appear phosphorescent, as in the Pikeperch. This phosphorescence enables the fishes to see more easily even in slightly cloudy water.

The difference in the size of the fish eye is immediately noticeable. Trout, Minnows, Perch and Pike have large eyes; Catfish, Horned Pout, Tench and other species have very small eyes. It has been proved that the size of the eye is proportional to the fish's vision. Fishes can be divided into diurnal (for example the Pike, Trout, Perch, Minnow, Three-spined Stickleback, Bitterling and Gudgeon) and nocturnal types (for example the Bream, Ruffe, Silver Bream, Eel, Barbel and Burbot). This division indicates the way of life of the above-named fishes, which are always more active at certain periods, and it is related also to the fish's vision.

All freshwater fishes can distinguish colour, although their ability to differentiate is not as high as the colour range of artificial baits would indicate. However, their colour vision is comparable to that of human beings. It enables the predator to recognize its camouflaged prey which blends with the surroundings, while the prey, because of the camouflage of the predator, can only discern it with the utmost difficulty. The fish with the sharpest sight in fresh water is the Pike, a voracious predator.

Hearing

It has long been debated whether fishes can hear or whether they are deaf. Experiments have been conducted during which fishes learnt to swim to the place where they were fed in response to sound stimuli. Even blind fishes learnt to do this. The hearing organ consists of an internal ear, a membranous sac enclosed by a bony casing. The cavity of this labyrinth is filled with a fluid, in which are located calcareous concretions, namely otoliths, by which incidentally it is also possible to establish the age of the fish.

In some species of fish, such as the Carp and Catfish, the hearing organ is connected to the air-bladder by a system of so-called Weber's bones. The changes in the size of the bladder arising from depth variations are, with the help of this system, reconciled by the membranous labyrinth, acting as the balance mechanism.

Smell and Taste

In fishes, the sense of smell, which has similarly been hotly disputed, is related to the existence of nostrils, formed by two olfactory cavities. With their help fishes can distinguish very accurately between bitter

33

and sweet matter. The sensory cells in the oral cavity and the skin are also helpful. Anglers exploit this fact to the full when fishing for Bream, Roach, Rudd and Carp and add various flavourings to the bread paste used for bait.

The olfactory cells are usually densely concentrated in the apertures by the nasal barbels near the mouth. By means of these barbels the fish is able to investigate large areas of the river bed. Long barbels, such as those of the Catfish, are definitely not used to entice prey into its mouth. The number of barbels is also a characteristic feature, important in distinguishing different species. For example the Catfish has six barbels, while the Horned Pout has eight. Sometimes they can be very small, as those of the Carp, Tench, Gudgeon, or larger and more prominent as those of the Barbel. A characteristic of all the Cod family is the one tentacle in the centre of the lower jaw. Smell and taste may also play an important part in the orientation of some members of the Salmon family when they return to their native streams.

The Skin

The skin is all important for the protection of the fish's body. It protects the fish from damage and it enables it to live in water. The outer layer of skin is the epidermis which is itself composed of several layers and under which there is a large number of cells secreting a slimy mucus, which helps the fish to overcome water resistance. The smaller the number of fish scales the greater the amount of slime produced. In some cases the epidermis can become very hard and a number of large and small protuberances, known as spawning rash, are formed in the Carp family. These eruptions are usually spread regularly over the head and the upper part of the body and they seldom cross the lateral line. In Roach, Bream and other fishes they make it easier to distinguish sex. They generally appear in the spawning season on the males only, seldom on the females where they are very faint if they do appear. The inner layer of the skin under the epidermis is called the dermis. Amongst other things, its importance for the fish lies in the fact that the scales start growing at this point.

It may be of interest to anglers to know that in the fish's skin the centres of the poisonous glands can be located near the spiky rays of the dorsal and pectoral fins, for example in the Horned Pout. When taking hold of the Horned Pout, it is essential to avoid injury that may be caused by the strong movements of its slimy body, as the secretion from its poisonous glands can cause inflammation.

The Scales, the Growth and the Age of Fishes

The scales are a characteristic part of the fish's body. They usually cover only the trunk of the fish, but in some species they can also cover the head or the caudal or other fins. Their function is mainly protective; they form the armour of the fish's body which reduces the risk of injury and the activity of various external parasites. However, their significance is much greater than this. With their help it is possible to establish the fish's age, the nature of its growth and to judge the nutritional value of the water.

The Scales

The structure and the arrangement of the scales on the fish's body varies in different species. The rhomboid bony scales of the Sturgeon form several rows and differ in origin and shape. The scales of freshwater fishes, described in this book, are very thin and generally arranged in slanting rows. The front end of each scale is set deep in the dermis and is covered by the hinder portion of the preceding scale. The arrangement of scales like roofing tiles would in itself prevent the fish from moving. Therefore the number of rows of scales usually corresponds to the number of muscle segments and vertebrae.

The fry, when hatched from the spawn, are completely naked; they have no scales. These start to form later and their appearance is related to the particular size of the fry in each species. As a rule, fishes with large scales start to develop them earlier; for example Carp fry develop them when they are 20 mm long, while fishes with small scales develop them later, for example the Pike and the Brown Trout develop them when their length is 40 mm.

If the Perch or Pikeperch is stroked from the tail to the head, the roughness of the body is at once apparent. On the other hand the surface of some fishes, such as Carp, Roach and Bream, is completely smooth. Rough

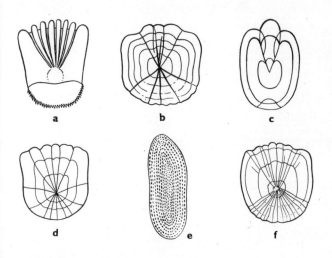

3. *The different shapes of fish scales*
a) Perch, b) Rudd, c) Pike, d) Crucian Carp, e) Eel, f) Carp

scales are characteristic of members of the Perch family. Such roughness is caused by a number of small, almost microscopic spines on the hinder edges of the scales. These scales are called ctenoid scales. The remaining species have smooth circular scales with spineless hind parts. These are cycloid scales and are typical of the Carp and Salmon families.

The Number of Scales in the Lateral Line

The number of scales in the lateral line is a conspicuous identifying characteristic of fishes with scale-covered bodies. The following table is a summary of the number of scales in specific lateral lines. The number fluctuates as shown and varies according to the fish species.

Salmon	114—130
Sea Trout	118—120
Brown Trout	115—132
Rainbow Trout	120—150
Charr	130—140
Alpine Charr	190—220
Brook Trout	109—130
Huchen	180—200
Whitefish	70— 91
Freshwater Houting	95—100
Houting	84—100
Grayling	74— 96
Pike	121—144
Roach	38— 49

Chub	44— 46
Orfe	56— 61
Dace	45— 55
Alburnoides bipunctatus	44— 51
Minnow	80— 92
Rudd	38— 42
Asp	65— 70
Tench	87—115
Gudgeon	40— 45
Nase	56— 63
Bitterling	4— 7
Bleak	42— 52
Barbel	56— 60
Silver Bream	43— 51
Bream	51— 60
Abramis ballerus	66— 73
Vimba vimba	56— 64
Pelecus cultratus	90—115
Crucian Carp	28— 33
Carp	30— 40
Large-mouth Bass	62— 68
Pumpkinseed	40— 47
Pikeperch	80— 97
Eastern Pikeperch	70— 83
Perch	62— 74
Zingel zingel	83— 95
Zingel streber	70— 82
Ruffe (Pope)	35— 40
Gymnocephalus schraetzer	55— 62

The Growth of Fishes

The scales increase in size as the fish grows. Around the base of each scale new lamellae called sclerites grow all the time. When looking at a scale, these are discernible as a number of dark and light rings arranged concentrically. They are reminiscent of the yearly growth rings of a tree. However, individual lamellae do not represent single years as they grow irregularly, depending on the fish's rate of growth. During the course of a year, when the fish is growing quickly (for example in the period of intensive feeding in summer) broad lamellae grow, whereas in the period of barely perceptible growth (for example in the Carp during winter) narrow lamellae develop. Similar alternation of dark and light zones can also be noticed in some fish bones, the opercular bones, the vertebrae and also the otoliths. The scales, bones and otoliths are useful for research into the speed of growth and the age of fishes. A detailed examination of a scale of a Carp, Pike, Bream, Chub and others under a magnifying glass can establish the age of the fish, since the winter and summer growth zones can be counted.

An examination of fish scales can also provide further information. Near the centre of the Salmon's scale there is an area with two to three narrow lamellae, which is a sign of the time spent in fresh water, when the Salmon was growing relatively slowly. This zone is adjacent to wider lamellar rings, which bear evidence of the length of life at sea, when the Salmon eats intensively and grows very quickly. Upon entering

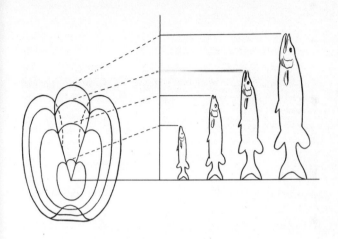

4. The growth of a fish scale is dependent on the growth in length of the fish. Yearly growth in the Pike's scales is closely related to its length.

the river, the Salmon swims upstream to the spawning grounds and during this time does not eat at all. After spawning and the return trip to the sea it quickly recuperates and starts growing again. The Salmon's scale therefore reveals not only the number of years spent in fresh water and at sea, but also indicates the number of spawnings.

The speed of the fish's growth varies according to environment, although quite often two fishes caught in the same environment and in the same place do not grow at the same speed. Knowledge of growth and weight increase is of great economic importance, since with the help of this data the nutritional value of the habitat can be assessed. As a matter of interest a table with the average length (in centimetres) of the fish's body relative to age is appended. The selected fishes include the types most often met in fishing. The age of scaleless fishes has been established from the growth zones of the opercular bones, the vertebrae or the otoliths.

Fish species	Age in years:							
	1	2	3	4	5	6	7	8
Sterlet (*U.S.S.R.*)	—	—	27	32	33	36	40	43
Salmon (*Denmark*)	14	20	60	80	95	—	—	—
Sea Trout (*Germany*)	14	44	57	68	73	—	—	—
Brown Trout (*averages from several localities*)	6	17	24	27	33	—	—	—
Huchen (**Lc, Slovakia*)	13	30	42	50	57	66	69	—
Grayling (*Bohemia*)	14	23	29	33	39	—	—	—
Pike (*Lc, England*) females	23	40	56	65	71	77	82	85
males	23	40	52	59	64	67	70	72

---

*Lc (*longitudo corporis*) represents the body length without tail. The remaining data indicate the total length of a fish. Measurements are stated in centimetres.

Fish species	Age in years:							
	1	2	3	4	5	6	7	8
Roach (Germany)	4	7	9	12	15	17	20	21
Chub (Lc, Czechoslovakia)	5	9	13	16	19	21	—	—
Crucian Carp (Lc, a slow grower, Bohemia)	3	4	5	—	7	8	9	11
(a fast grower, U.S.S.R.)	4	11	13	15	18	—	—	—
Carp (Lc, Europe)	4-13	15-25	19-33	25-38	27-42	—	—	—
European Catfish (Czechoslovakia)	11-14	24-33	36-50	49-65	60-76	70-86	84-93	—
European Eel (Germany)	9	12	15	19	25	31	35	39
Pikeperch (Germany)	14	25	38	48	51	57	61	—
Perch (Europe, average)	7	11	13	15	17	18	21	—

The Age of Fishes

Until recently it was not completely clear, how long fishes can live. Theories about the longevity of some fishes stood for a long time, involving claims that they can survive several human generations. It has been stated that Carp can live 250 to 300 years. According to one legend an 'Emperor's Pike', which was caught in Würtemberg in the year 1497, was put into the water with a lead mark by Frederick II himself in A.D. 1230. In reality its skeleton in Mannheim cathedral is composed of several large Pike.

Freshwater fishes do not live to an old age. The Sterlet can live to the age of 24 years. The age of fishes in many cases depends on size. The smallest fishes live short lives; for example the Three-spined Stickleback and the Bitterling live 3 years and the Gudgeon and Ruffe 6 years. Of the large fishes, the Carp lives up to 17 years, the Pike between 11 and 14 years, the Roach and Perch up to 16 years, and the Grayling 7 years. The environment of the fish must not be forgotten in connection with age. In vast areas of water with little fishing and suitable living conditions, there is every opportunity for large fishes to live to a ripe old age. The reverse is true in enclosed waters that are heavily fished. Given the current developments in angling and the modernization of fishing techniques, fishes have a small chance of living to an old age and growing to a large size.

Fishes and the Water Environment

The Shape of the Fish's Body

The great variety in body shape of fishes is caused by variation in the water environment and the slow evolution of these vertebrates. It would be difficult to describe the variety in the body shape of fishes. However, for our purpose it will be sufficient to mention the fishes met with when fishing in running or still, fresh water.

The most common is the torpedo-shaped body, typical of good swimmers, which are usually predators and able to follow their prey swiftly over long distances. In cross-section, the body of this shape-type is circular. The fins are evenly developed, so that the body is not needlessly resistant to strong-flowing water (for example Salmon and Trout). This shape is less common among non-predatory fishes and is limited to the good swimmers (for example Chub and Dace). It can be said without reservation that all fishes with this type of body, sometimes called spindle-shaped or cigar-like, are efficient and fast swimmers.

Disc-shaped fishes can generally be found in quiet waters, either still or slow running. It is typical of various fishes of the Carp family, such as the Bream, the Silver Bream and the Crucian Carp. The body of such fishes is vertically flattened at the sides. The disc-shaped body is also common to fishes living near the bottom; their body is flattened dorsoventrally, that is from the dorsal and ventral parts, as in Catfish and the Horned Pout. Disc-shaped fishes usually over-develop one pair of fins which they adapt for clinging purposes. There is a number of stages between torpedo and disc shapes, for example the Houting's body is elongated and is deeper than it is wide, so that the cross-section of the body is oval.

5. Different body shapes of fishes are characteristic of their way of life in water.

Sturgeon family
Acipenseridae

Salmon family
Salmonidae

Grayling family
Thymallidae

Pike family
Esocidae

Carp family
Cyprinidae

The bodies of some fishes such as the Eel, are cylindrical with a circular cross-section. This fish is typical of the animal life on the bed of river or lake. The fins are adjusted to the sinuous movements of the body and in shape resemble a long fringe.

Catfish family
Siluridae

North-American Catfish family
Ictaluridae

Eel family
Anguillidae

Cod family
Gadidae

Perch family
Percidae

47

The Shape of the Head and the Caudal Fin

The shape of the fish's head is also indicative of its way of life. The fish's mouth, its shape and position, correspond to its method of feeding and the nature of its normal diet. The mouth of a fish feeding on plankton (Herring, Houting and some of the Carp family) is of medium size, does not usually protrude and has small or no teeth at all. The suctorial mouth is of a different shape: it is shaped like a tube and sometimes it sticks out. The fish uses it to suck organisms from the bottom. It is characteristic of Sturgeon and the Bream. The mouth of typical predators, such as the Pike and Catfish, can open very wide and is armed with strong and diversely toothed jaws; this is called a snapping mouth.

The mouths of fishes can be categorized according to their position.

The upper position of the mouth (the Bleak) indicates that food is being collected from the water surface or from the top layer of water. The Nase has a low-positioned mouth and lives on algal growths scraped off stones. Carp, Roach and Chub have terminal or centrally positioned mouths. Apart from this, there are many other shapes of fish mouth. Sea fishes are particularly noted for the numerous differences and peculiarities of their mouths.

As with the body and the head, the caudal fin's variety of shape is also considerable.

The Salmon's and the Trout's caudal fins have a straight cut, whereas in different representatives of the Carp family they are symmetrically curved. In

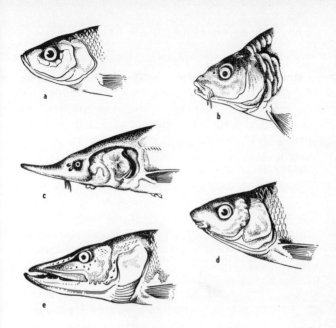

6. *Various types of mouth position are as follows:*

a) *upper position of the mouth (Pelecus cultratus)*
b) *terminal position of the mouth (Carp)*
c) *lower position of the mouth (Sturgeon)*
d) *the horny mouth of Chondrostoma nasus, which is used to
   scrape food (algae) off hard surfaces.*
e) *the full mouth of predatory fish (Pike)*

Burbot they curve outwards, in Sturgeon they are asymmetrical, the top lobe slanting upwards and being elongated. The shape of the caudal fin is determined by the shape of the caudal section of the spine.

The Changing Colours of Fishes

The beautiful colours of the fish's body, particularly the male's during the spawning season, are well known to anglers. The colouring changes not only during the course of a single year, but is also influenced by the psychological condition of the fish and by its environment. Colour variability is caused by the presence of pigment cells in the skin, namely chromatophores; of these, melanophores produce a black pigment, erythrophores a red one, and xanthophores a yellow one, while guanophores, containing crystals of guanine, known as fish silver, cause the silvery sheen of some species.

The Trout, when removed from water, is ablaze with colour. When put in a container with a light bottom, it changes its coloration in several minutes; its body turns lighter and the colours blend together. The melanophores can contract during a change of environment, making the body lighter, or they can expand so that the body becomes darker. Other pigment cells' reaction is similar.

In some fishes, apart from black, red, yellow and silver colours, blues and greens can also be found. The origin of these colours is explained by the reflection and passage of light rays through several of the above pigment cells. Blues are caused by the rays passing through melanophores, guanophores and xanthophores. In such cases the fish's eyes are a regulating factor of great significance, for example a blind Pike's colouring is always black, although the exact cause of this phenomenon is not clear.

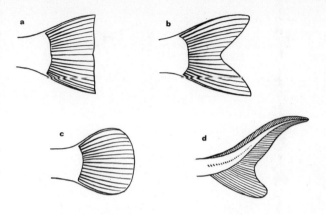

7. Various shapes of caudal fins:
a) straight cut, b) curved, c) rounded, d) asymmetrical

The exceptions to usual fish colours are rare, but all the same they exist. Tench, Crucian Carp, and Orfe with a gold coloration are bred in the small ponds and reservoirs in parks This phenomenon is called xanthorism, if the fish has black eyes. A very different case is albinism, caused by the absence of pigment, apart from the silvery one, and in this case the fish's eyes are red.

The whole range of colours and shades, characteristic of certain species of fish, is only evident in living fishes, freshly caught in their natural environment. All species adjust themselves to the colour conditions and environmental differences, namely to the character of the bottom. In this way colouring carries out a protective function, that is, it provides camouflage

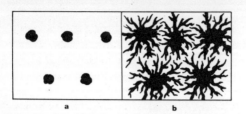

8. The pigment cells, melanophores, present in the fish's skin:
a) the fish cells on a light background
b) the change in cell shape brought about by the change of a light
background to a dark one.

against predators. These colour changes are best
illustrated by Carp or Trout taken from wooded or
shaded ponds, where the colouring of both types is
very dark, nearly black, and contrasts sharply with the
light coloration of those living in sunny, open ponds or
streams with clay bottoms. That is why the Trout is
sometimes called the fish chameleon. The water
temperature, the amount of oxygen, the pellucidity
and light intensity are also relevant to changes in the
colour of the fish's skin.

A thin Trout caught in a sparse environment is
usually dark in colour. This is explained by the fact
that during starvation the fat reserves are used up and
the functioning of the yellow pigment cells is dependent on the presence of fat. Other circumstances, such
as injury, the presence of parasites and infectious
disease can also cause certain parts of a fish's body to
turn black. Colour changes are further conditioned by
nervous shocks and internal gland secretion, which

causes a colour change in the male during the spawning season.

Colour plays an appreciable role in the life of fishes. It has been shown that through colour changes fishes transmit information about reproduction, food, defence and gathering in shoals. Finally fishes surpass many other animals in the beauty and gaiety of their colouring.

Different Living Conditions and the Needs of Fishes

Fishes have been adjusting themselves to the living conditions of their environment throughout the long process of evolution. Only those species survived which were able to adapt themselves; the rest gradually died out. Environmental influence is evident from the habitat of individual species of freshwater fishes. The slope of the bed is crucially important, as is the speed of the flow, the amount of oxygen and the temperature of the water. The oxygen content of water in mountainous areas does not fluctuate during the course of the year and temperatures keep within certain limits, seldom exceeding 10°C. Fishes from this zone, in particular the Trout, are distinguished by their muscular bodies, which are resistant to fast-flowing water. Fishes of the Salmon family and the Alpine Bullhead belong to this group.

In places, where the flow slows down, the water is still relatively cold; it hardly exceeds 18°C in the course of a whole year and always has an adequate oxygen content. This sub-mountainous zone has, as its typical inhabitant the Grayling, although it is not always present there in great numbers. There is a gradual transition between the two zones, arising from man's interference with the natural environment, as in the artificial regulation of the river, so that the zones lose their distinctive identity. Trout waters can develop in the lower reaches of the river, below a dam, which often releases cold water at the bottom. Here important food items are insect larvae and other organisms of the river bottom.

Barbel and Chub like to stay in places where the meandering river has formed muddy deposits on its shoulders and banks. This zone is also inhabited by large predatory fishes, such as Pike and Perch, which frequent the river's quieter stretches and its sides.

In valleys, the river nearly comes to a halt in some places and the surface becomes overgrown in parts by water vegetation. The water temperature markedly varies during the year as does the oxygen content of the water. Plankton always plays a significant role in the fish's diet in such a place. However, the bottom is usually soft with a sufficient amount of food for members of the Carp family and here plankton is a less important source of fish food. One of the numerous fishes at this level is the Bream. Also plentiful are Silver Bream, Roach, Rudd, Ruffe, and the predatory types are represented by Pike, Perch, and Catfish.

It is difficult to differentiate still waters in a similar way. It is commonly accepted that living conditions are more stable the larger and deeper the expanse of water. The decisive factors, which give the zones their respective individuality, are the nature of the vegetation, the composition of the bottom, the depth, and the variety of invertebrates. At the river estuaries, fresh water and sea water merge into the brackish zones, where it is possible to find fishes typical of fresh waters and also marine species, which inhabit coastal areas.

Migration and the Change in the Location of Fishes

When fishing in rivers and even great stretches of water, it can happen that the fishes are not biting. There can be several reasons for this, but the most common cause is usually the fact that the fishes have moved away. Generally speaking fishes migrate to places with more advantageous living conditions. As a result much discussion takes place about migration to the spawning grounds and the search for food. Several species of fish living in fresh waters travel long distances from the sea to spawn, for example the Salmon, the Sea Trout and the Sturgeon, and the reverse is true that some fishes travel from fresh waters to the sea, for example the Eel. Fishermen must appreciate such distinctive ways of life, especially in large lakes and rivers, where fishing has a significant economic value.

The migration of fishes is investigated by marking them beforehand. Labels or tubes with a serial number and other data are fixed by rust-proof wires or nylon fibres to the hard fin rays or other parts of a fish's body. The measurements of the fish, the date and place of release are recorded. With the help of such marking

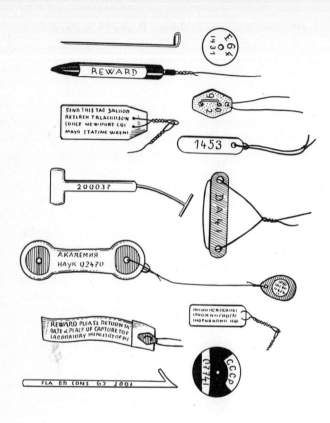

9. Different types of fish markings used in studying the migration of fishes.

techniques it is possible to trace the movement of fishes and find out the number living in reservoirs or rivers and the death rate. Nevertheless marking methods still pose a problem. Research workers have tried chemical and thermal methods, tattooing and cauterising some fishes and colouring their fry with distinctive colours. Radioactive techniques have also been tried. In some cases the marks are worked deep into the skin or into the muscle and are subsequently located by magnets. Marking has helped to determine the static nature of many species. A marked Pike was caught several times and released in the same place and did not change its location for several successive years. Many fishes, such as the Bream, can return to their original habitat despite being relocated elsewhere. It is interesting to follow the greatest traveller of all fishes, namely the Eel. During its life it has to undertake two long journeys. The first one takes place after hatching out in the sea, when the larva travels 4,000 to 5,000 miles across the Atlantic Ocean to European rivers and the second one back to the sea after an interval of about 10 years. In fresh water the Eel settles down in one place and usually lives in it or in its vicinity for many years.

Fishes and Food

Some fish species will eat various types of food and on occasion accept a completely different diet. However, predatory fishes generally live on large, living organisms while non-predators feed on plant fragments, algae and invertebrates.

Fishes can starve for a long time, up to several months, and live on the fat reserves stored in the liver, muscles and the ventral cavity. To find out what a fish lives on in a strange environment, its stomach or the front part of the intestine of stomachless fishes must be examined.

When Fishes Eat

It is an instinctive desire of all anglers to know the exact time when fishes accept food. The problem depends on various factors and it is not easy or even possible to give a precise answer. Experiments with small Perch living on plankton indicated that in summer at a water temperature of 21°C food acceptance is lowest between 7 p.m. and 3 a.m. After sunrise the feeding intensity started rising and reached a peak around 11 a.m. This outline is a general indicator for fishes feeding on plankton and is accounted for by the rising activity of plankton organisms as daylight breaks on the water surface. Experienced anglers would agree that it is usually hopeless to try to catch fishes feeding on plankton at night. Experiments with Perch living on bottom-dwelling organisms show that the highest intake of food is between 7 a.m. and 5 p.m. Both groups of Perch do not feed at night.

In contrast Burbot and Eels react differently to the fading daylight. Both types are more active in looking for food as night falls and they stop eating at dawn. This knowledge is used for catching Eels en masse, the fishes being driven by batteries of lights to dark places, in which the traps are set. It follows that when fishing for Burbot and Eels, the results are better during dark nights than during the full moon phase or in the daytime. However, the light of a fire does not repel Burbot.

The reaction of the fishes to light, whether positive or negative, is a result of some inherited defensive features. The fish fry stay near the water surface, where they find sufficient oxygen and food and try to hide away from pursuing predators. Generally speaking, their positive reaction, or movement towards light, is common to all species living off plankton, which they locate with the help of their sight and the light. In contrast, species feeding on the bottom, such as the Eel, react to light in an opposite manner. The majority of fishes, especially those dependent on sight when searching for food, start to feed in the early hours of the morning and, if they are not satisfied, they continue feeding all day. Daybreak is a signal for them to start feeding. However, light has ceased to act as a signal for species which are not dependent on sight in their quest for food. Finally light also helps the majority of fishes to orientate themselves spatially.

The Food of Small Fishes

Almost all small species of fish and all fry of predatory and non-predatory fishes live on small aquatic animals, usually planktonic crustaceans. They can be found in still waters and in slow-running streams, quite often in shallow water, in flooded undergrowth and among water plants, which in effect means everywhere small fishes and the fry of large fishes live. The amount of plankton in a certain volume of water can be easily ascertained by pouring a given amount of water through a fine net.

The most prolific types of such small species are *Daphnia, Cyclops* and *Diaptomus*. The last two representatives can be identified by their long, segmented bodies. The females have one or two egg pouches. They travel in water with peculiar jerky movements. *Cyclops* feed like predators, while *Daphnia* and *Diaptomus* filter algae and fragments of green plants. The minute fry eat small freshly hatched larvae and Rotifers of many types and sizes.

The Food of Non-predatory Fishes

The fauna at the bottom of still waters consists of larger organisms. These are temporary water residents and include the larvae and the pupae of water insects, above all midge larvae. Permanent inhabitants are worms and molluscs. The number of individual types fluctuates during the course of a year. They are most numerous on the bottom in autumn and winter and at their most sparse towards the end of spring and in summer. Such variations are caused by insect life cycles, since when the larvae mature they change into pupae and leave the water as mature insects. In the second half of summer and in autumn a new generation of young bottom-living organisms arrives and the cycle is repeated. The majority of insects hibernating in water do so as larvae, which explains their prevalence in autumn and winter. Changes in the number of insects are caused by large numbers of fishes living on the bottom-dwelling organisms. Primarily the midge larvae, which live on the surface of the water bed are eaten, followed by the worms that live deeper. Many midges are eaten in the pupal stage, during their time below the water surface, prior to emerging as fully fledged insects.

The situation is different in fast-flowing waters. Bottom-living organisms can be found floating here or attached to one spot. The first group is formed by the larvae of the Mayfly, the Stonefly, and some Caddis Flies and by the Shrimp; the second group is represented by the larvae of other types of Caddis Fly, and of *Odagmia* and by molluscs. Plentiful supplies of larvae and fishes are found in places with large stones rather than in areas with a sandy bottom, which do not provide the fishes with either food or a hideout. The majority of larvae lie under stones, a fact which can be easily proved by turning them over carefully.

Suitable bait for catching fishes is to be found in such places.

The Food of Predatory Fishes

Tall stories have been told about the amount of food eaten by a Pike or a Catfish. Such stories suggest that they need an amount of food every day which is equivalent to their own weight. This would mean that a 2 lb Pike eats about 700 lb of small fishes per year, a fact which, if true, would quickly lead to the disappearance of fishes from the waters where Pike live. In fact, for a 2 lb increase in weight, all predators, not only Pike, need 8 to 12 lb of food. This amount varies and depends on the body measurements of the predator, on the reserves of food and the temperature of the environment. The warmer the water is, the quicker the digestive process is and vice versa. Only during hot summer days, when the temperature rises to 30°C, can feeding be stopped temporarily. A smaller predator has a smaller consumption and accordingly a smaller weight increase. Large fishes eat more and increase their weight faster; it is not unusual for a large Catfish to put on 2 to 6 lb a year. The only fish species in the fresh waters of northern Europe to break this rule is the Burbot, which, as the water gradually gets colder, starts eating larger amounts of food. Pike, Perch and Pikeperch also feed in cold conditions or in winter, but the amount is always smaller than in summer. A good catch of Pike in autumn is indicative of the lack of small fishes near the shore at this time.

The speed of the digestive process of predatory fishes is not the same in all species. It is impossible to say how long a predator remains full after catching its prey. The satiation time changes during the course of a year and is firmly related to the speed of the digestive process and the temperature of the water. The secretion rate of the gastric juices also varies according to the water temperature. The general rule for the majority of predatory fishes is that the rate of digestion increases with a rising temperature and vice versa. Large Perch digest fry in 10 hours 30 minutes at a temperature of 24°C, while at a temperature of 1 to 2°C they take about 6 days which is some thirteen times slower. The angler can easily relate this fact to the context of his own experience, although other circumstances play an important part here. In summer with favourable temperatures producing a fast digestion rate, Perch still have a surplus of food. In addition they are widely dispersed in the water, along with their food. Large catches therefore cannot be anticipated, especially from fishing in one place. It is often maintained, that fishes are not biting at a particular time but in fact this is not always true. On the contrary during a cold season, when the digestive process has slowed down and feeding is limited, Perch gather in shoals and concentrate in certain places. If such a spot is found, a good catch can be expected even during seasons with adverse temperatures.

The time predators take to digest eaten fishes varies considerably and depends on the type of fish swallowed. The skin of Perch and Ruffe with its thick scales is more resistant to digestion than the skin of Roach or

Bleak, which can be digested considerably more quickly. The number of eaten fishes is also relevant. One or two fishes in the stomach are most easily digested, but when this number increases, the digestive process slows down. The size of the consumed fishes has a similar significance. It has been realized from lengthy observation, that the majority of predatory fishes have only one or two small fishes in their digestive organs, although exceptions are quite common; for example the Burbot usually eats more of them. The size of the predator also plays a part, as larger fishes digest more slowly than smaller fishes. It is of interest that Pike-perch and Perch digest more quickly than Pike. It can be concluded from this that in a given place with a given equal number of the above mentioned predators, Pikeperch and Perch are more likely to be caught than Pike.

The Burbot differs from other fishes in the way in which temperature influences its digestive process. It digests more slowly as the temperature of the environment increases, more quickly when the water is colder. This fact is consistent with its special biological make-up, which is adapted to the conditions of the polar regions.

The Pike—the Most Common Predatory Fish

A study of the Pike makes it easier to understand the particular nature of the food of predatory fishes. The Pike is the best known predator of inland waters. Some of its data is generally applicable to other predatory species, although most of them have certain individual characteristics related to their distinctive natures and also to their different environmental conditions. Until recently the Pike has been blamed for the disappearance of fishes from rivers and lakes, and so the length at which it could be killed was set very low, or in some places restrictions were almost non-existent. At present the Pike is not only valuable for its sporting potential, but also as an economically useful fish in eastern European fish ponds, which transforms the meat of small, economically unimportant types into a valuable product. It is located in still, fresh inland waters and its prevalence should be increased and promoted by all available means.

An examination of the contents of a number of Pike stomachs of various sizes from waters lacking Trout revealed that Pike live predominantly on small, insignificant types of fish. In places populated by such fishes, the largest part of the stomach's content (fifty to eighty per cent) is formed by Perch, Ruffe, Roach and Rudd. The basic constituent of the food of Pike, measuring up to 70 cm, is fishes with an average length of 70 mm. Although the size of the prey generally increases with the length of the predator, this is not always the case. For instance Perch longer than 12 cm are a rarity in the Pike's diet. The largest Pike usually eat only one fish, such as Roach, Bream, Carp or Pike. Because of their size, these are valuable fishes for sport and therefore large Pike, about 1 m long, are not welcomed in well-tended waters and it is best to get rid of them.

When hunting, the Pike uses its good sight for orientation and can recognize its prey at a distance of 2 to

2.5 m. Even a blind Pike can find food, by using its 'echo-location system', a series of openings in the lateral line, which guide it exactly to its prey. This predator can therefore feed at night, although it is considerably less active then. In fact the quantity of the food eaten at night only amounts to one quarter of the food eaten during the day.

The greatest number of fishes in the Pike's stomach can be found in the morning and in the evening, because its prey usually gathers in shoals at these times, and whereas the Pike's vision is good, the vision of small fishes is poor. During the course of the day there is often a certain fluctuation in the Pike's diet; subject to availability it tends to eat Carp fry predominantly in the morning, Perch all day and Ruffe in the evening, since at dusk the activity of Ruffe near the shore increases. To catch Pike with live fishes it is important to know that eighty per cent of fishes consumed by Pike are swallowed head first, a factor not to be forgotten when fixing live bait to the hook.

The Fishes and the Algae in the Water

Under suitable conditions algae can spread to the still waters of reservoirs, lakes and ponds to such an extent that the water is completely coloured green, yellowish-green or brownish-yellow. This often happens when small fishes, such as Perch and Roach, multiply profusely or the fry of large fishes become numerous. Both groups live on the animal plankton. Then if all plank-tonic crustaceans, which live on the algae, are eaten, the algae multiply swiftly and colour the water. Neither water board managers nor anglers are pleased with this fact. An abundant proliferation of algae indicates a shortage of predatory fishes and suggests that only those anglers specializing in catching small fishes will get any sport at all. Research shows that this always happens when there are more than 12,000 fishes in 1 acre of water in the reservoir. The pellucidity of such waters is low, only about 0.5 m. The specialist examining such water discovers that the planktonic organisms are very small, hardly 0.5 to 1 mm long. In places with a smaller proportion of fishes, about 280 to 1 acre, the water transparency is considerably higher. Planktonic animals in such waters grow larger, up to several millimetres in length.

The Smell of Mud

It often happens that freshwater fishes seem to smell of mud and the flesh is unpleasant to eat. What causes this muddy smell and the unpalatable nature of the flesh? A thorough study has revealed that such fishes live in waters inhabited by a large population of a kind of blue-green alga, *Oscillatoria*. It forms microscopic fibres and multiplies during warm summer days. It thrives in the muddy areas of the rivers where open sewers emit human and food waste. Predatory fishes, living on small fishes with *Oscillatoria* in their digestive organs, not unnaturally smell too. Fishermen near such places quite rightly complain about the quality of the fishes caught. Hence it is inadvisable to fish in such an environment with open sewers both from hygienic and aesthetic points of view.

The Effect of Algal Blooms

During warm summer days in optimal living conditions for the development of algae, the surface of the reservoir can become covered with an opaque layer. Upon seeing such a carpet, the angler usually departs in a disgruntled mood for he knows from experience that the fishes do not bite in such conditions. This phenomenon is caused by the over production of algae and anglers often call it 'water bloom'. However, anglers cannot explain why fishes do not bite in such circumstances. In places where the wind has blown the algae inshore, a thick, pulpish green mass is found, which in time decomposes and smells strongly. The chemical change in the water environment is the main unfavourable consequence for fishes. The oxygen and carbon dioxide content and the acidity of the water (pH) markedly fluctuate during the day and night in such places. The algae grow quickly, die off and sink to the bottom, where they decompose and absorb a large quantity of oxygen from the water. Fishes usually leave such places and under such circumstances it is best to try fishing near the water surface or in places where the wind has blown the algae away.

Artificial Bait

The effectiveness of artificial bait on predators was scientifically tested out on various species of both sea and freshwater fishes. It was established that the shape of artificial bait can vary. Decisive factors for success are always good visibility and mobility in the water. That is why artificial bait is usually golden or silvery in colour and spins; in this connection spinning lures are very effective. An important aspect of successful fishing with artificial bait is the slow sideways movement of the offered bait, which allows the Pike to give chase. However, it is not difficult to catch Perch when the lure or other bait is retrieved vertically, as for instance from a boat or from the ice, because this fish is accustomed to chase its prey from the bottom towards the water surface and catch it there. Experiments have been conducted with Perch in ponds, during which they were hooked several times and then put back. After being caught several times they stopped reacting to the bait. Subsequently in the course of two ensuing years nobody managed to catch a Perch, although they were still there when the water from the pond was drained away.

Catching non-predatory fishes with artificial bait is limited by many factors. The colours of the bait, its size, shape and taste play an important part. Generally speaking non-predatory fishes react better to offered food which is moving slowly, while predatory types are more attracted by fast-moving bait. It is possible to define types of movement and say that fishes of the former group react principally to worm-like movements and predators to jerky, interrupted and sharp movements. Anglers fishing for predatory species would usually agree that a jerky sideways movement of the lure excites all types of predators. In conclusion, when fishing with artificial bait, the way in which the bait is moved and its size are decisive, not its shape or colour. This has been proved on many occasions and such knowledge is extremely valuable for anglers. Unfortunately it is not sufficiently put into practice.

The Sterlet

Acipenser ruthenus

Sturgeon family

Acipenseridae

The Acipenseridae family, which is grouped in the order Chondrostei of cartilaginous fishes, is not very numerous; it includes twenty-three species. They are usually semi-migratory and migratory fishes, living in the northern temperate zone. Their body is spindle-shaped with five surface rows of bony plates.

The Sterlet has a long snout with four frilly barbels. During warm weather it can be found in shallow waters and in streams, whereas in winter it hides in deep water. In contrast to other Sturgeons it lives exclusively in fresh water. It inhabits the rivers and their tributaries which flow into the Black, Azov and Caspian Seas. It does not reach large proportions; it grows to a weight of 2 to 4 lb, although in exceptional circumstances it may weigh more than this; it lives 10 to 20 years. It reaches central Europe via the Danube from which it penetrates other tributaries. Breeding takes place at the end of spring in fast-flowing parts of the river and preferably close to sandy islands.

When fishing, Sterlet can be found in deep, fast-flowing water. Fishing for Sterlet is similar to catching Barbel, which live in the same stretches of the river. Fishing is usually successful early in the morning or in the early evening and goes on until late at night. Different types of fleshy bait, such as earthworms and larvae can be used. The Sterlet grips the bait in its funnel-like mouth very gently. To hook the fish in time and at the right moment it is advisable to hold the rod all the time. Once hooked, the Sterlet puts up a good fight and often jumps out of the water, but usually the hook remains firm in its very fleshy mouth. It can tolerate being out of water and a fortunate angler can carry it live, over short distances, in a damp cloth. Its flesh has a pleasant flavour.

Acipenser ruthenus

The Common Sturgeon

Acipenser sturio

Sturgeon family

Acipenseridae

At present this fish is the only representative of the Sturgeon family in western Europe. It differs from other types of Sturgeon in its thick roughened skin. The mouth with its split lower lip is in the typical inferior position. The dorsal fin, as in the Sterlet, is positioned close to the start of the anal fin. It differs from the previous species in the number of bony plates on its back and sides.

It is another Sturgeon with a wide-ranging habitat. It used to be widespread in the hinterland of the Baltic Sea, in the Gulf of Finland. At present it can also be found in the northern part of the Atlantic Ocean, off the European and American coastline and in the Mediterranean and Black Seas. It is generally a solitary fish, but moves up river in shoals to breed. At sea it undertakes long journeys as far as the shores of Tunisia. It has been asserted that the Common Sturgeon grows to a length of 3 m and a weight of 700 lb, but even a fish weighing 200 lb is generally thought to be an exceptional catch. In fact it usually weighs only 40 to 80 lb. It lives to a good age, up to 40 years. Formerly it used to enter many European rivers, including the Elbe and others from the North Sea, but nowadays it is becoming rarer as a result of the pollution of European fresh waters and the numerous hydrotechnical installations being built.

In the spawning season the females, depending on the size of the fish, lay 200,000 to 5,500,000 eggs. The fry float slowly towards the sea with the current. Experiments in breeding the Common Sturgeon in special hatcheries and then putting it into the rivers have been successful. The Common Sturgeon is usually caught in a net, rarely on a hook because of its scarcity. Its flesh is very tasty and boneless; it is delicious when smoked. Their roe is used for the production of caviar.

Acipenser sturio

The Salmon
Salmo salar

Salmon family
Salmonidae

This fish is a typical representative of the Salmon family (Salmonidae). A characteristic feature of all representatives of this family is their torpedo-shaped body, which is typical of good swimmers. Its external appearance, coloration and the quality of its flesh justify its pre-eminent position among fishes. Apart from its lines of scales and its fin rays, the plowshare bone (or the vomer), situated at the top of the jaw cavity, is its important distinctive feature. The Salmon inhabits the northern part of the Atlantic Ocean from the river Pechora (U.S.S.R.) to the Portuguese river Duero, the east coast of Canada, Greenland, Iceland and Britain. It is distinguished from its relative, the Sea Trout, by its emarginate caudal fin and dark spots on its head and the upper half of the body. The silvery scales flake away slightly. The male's body is slimmer and its lower jaw is bent in the shape of a hook, particularly in older fishes.

During the breeding season the Salmon moves well up into the rivers, and this does not always take place at the same time of the year. In the Scottish rivers, migration starts as early as March, while in Ireland it starts mainly in June. Sometimes two generations, differing in size, migrate to the same river, one in spring and one in autumn. The main migration, characterized by the Salmon leaping out of the water, begins in spring, when the water temperature rises above 6°C. Fishes moving up river in autumn, usually spawn in the lower reaches of the rivers and their tributaries, whereas the spring migration takes them to the river's source. At this time the silvery shade of the Salmon's body darkens and their red flesh becomes pale pink and less tasty. Spawning takes place during the winter months on gravel or rough,

Salmo salar—male

The Salmon
continued

sandy water beds. The female cleans and prepares the area by digging small pits, where she lays 5,000 to 30,000 eggs, according to her size. Salmon weighing 10 to 20 lb spawn in water 15 to 60 cm deep, flowing at a speed of 30 to 45 cm per sec. At this time they often fall prey to poachers and various predators, such as the otter. The constant flow of the river provides a favourable oxygenated environment for the spawn while hatching. Many males die after spawning. The fry hatch in 100 to 150 days and they live in fresh water for 2 to 3 years (parr) and when the fishes reach 10 to 20 cm (smolt), they return to the sea. In colour the parr is similar to small Trout; it is the smolt that acquires the silvery sheen at the sides of the body, which is characteristic of Salmon.

On their way to the sea, some fishes are lost when they pass through polluted parts of the river or close to the turbines of power-stations. Fish ladders have therefore been built in the dams of some power-stations. In the sea the Salmon has a bountiful supply of food and it feeds voraciously for a period of 1 to 3 years. The males then return to fresh water earlier than the females. Weight increases of 4 to 11 lb per year are not rare, although more usual in females than males, and in this connection the length of stay at sea is a decisive factor. During the journey up river they do not feed at all, although judging from some hooked fishes, this seems difficult to believe. In view of the increasing number and variety of obstacles during the journey to the spawning grounds, Salmon are caught in special traps, transfered to hatcheries and are milted artificially. They are kept for 1 to 2 years in small concrete or earthen ponds and only then are they put back into the water.

Salmo salar—female

The Salmon

continued

In recent years Salmon have been plagued by a little known disease of the skin (necrosis), whose symptoms can be seen when the fish is in water. They take the form of a whitish coating of the head and other parts of the body. Places where Salmon breed regularly become a tourist attraction and it is a popular pastime to watch them leaping out of the water. Research has shown that a number of Salmon stay near the coast and the estuaries of their native rivers, while others undertake long journeys of up to 800 miles. At sea they can travel 20 to 60 miles in a day.

The Salmon is usually caught both by fresh bait (for example maggots and fish pieces) and artificial bait (for example spinners, plugs and flies). Fishing, generally using artificial bait, is of considerable economic importance to those countries which practise it (for example Sweden, Norway, Ireland and Scotland). A catch of a single Salmon on a hook can represent up to ten times as much profit as compared with that from netting a single Salmon at sea. Angling is responsible for the development of an industry producing angling tackle. Fishing with large flies, such as Durham Ranger, Jock Scott, Grey Turkey, Fiery Brown, Wilkinson and others is now considered a traditional method. Artificial 'shrimps' and 'insects' of a high quality are also produced. Various other baits, for example the Sand Eel Tail Spinner and bunches of artificial worms have also proved effective when fished on strong tackle. Angling using artificial lures (for example various types of Devon Minnow and fantastic combinations of flies and metal lures), requires quality tackle and a good landing net or gaff. Fishing for Salmon is definitely not easy for the beginner.

Salmo salar—detail of head

The Sea Trout

Salmon family

Salmo trutta trutta

Salmonidae

It is possible to find the Salmon and the Sea Trout in the same places. The Sea Trout can be met with near the northern coast of Europe, in the Baltic Sea, and off the shores of England, Scotland and Ireland. After hatching it stays for 2 to 3 years in fresh water. The majority of Sea Trout leave fresh water in the second and third year of their life. At sea, they inhabit areas adjacent to the estuaries of their native rivers. One of their individual traits is that they return to the place of their birth to spawn a new generation. Adult fishes are guided home by their taste and smell memory, being able to analyse their home waters. On their first return trip, fishes weighing 4 to 7 lb are usually caught. The oldest ones can be over 1 m long and weigh 35 lb. In Scotland and Ireland, Salmon and Sea Trout can often be seen together between May and July in the artificial fish ways. They can be distinguished by the shape of their caudal fin, which is truncate in the Trout and emarginate in the Salmon. The opercular bones are formed differently; they differ in the number of gill filaments, those of the Trout being fewer in number. The Salmon lacks the dark flecks under the lateral line that characterize the Sea Trout.

Sea Trout usually travel in shoals; sometimes they wait in the river mouth for warmer weather and they like to travel at night, too. It has been observed that moonlight influences their nocturnal activity, for example at full moon, instead of swimming against the flow of the river, they have been seen lying passively on the river bed. If they pass through a lake on their journey, they like to linger on its

Salmo trutta trutta—male

The Sea Trout

continued

sandy and gravel banks which they use as natural hideaways. In lochs in Scotland and Ireland, large Trout reappear after a four year period and similarly in Finland and Norway. The differences in size of fishes when leaving the sea and entering the rivers, are roughly the same as in Salmon and are caused by the inequalities of time spent in the sea, as some fishes return to the rivers after 12 months, and others after 2 to 3 years. Fast growth in the sea causes considerable differences in size although compared with the Salmon, the growth of the Trout in sea water is somewhat slower. Hence when small fishes have consistently been returning to the rivers, groups of local specialists have conducted experiments in the stricken areas and imported larger fishes from other regions, for example Trout from Poland have been imported into Ireland.

The Trout breeding season usually lasts from October until November. The female chooses a gravelly sandy bed, which she clears by sharp movements of her tail. After the shedding of 5,000 to 8,000 eggs, these eggs are fertilized by the male and the female tries to cover the spawn by restirring the sand and fine gravel. The spawn can easily be taken for that of the Brown Trout. These related species can easily be crossbred, as the Sea Trout laid the foundations for the present world population of Brown Trout. During the time at sea, the Trout lives on various small fishes or their fry, such as Herring, Sprat and various crustaceans. There are, however, known cases of groups settling in fresh water.

In places where the Sea Trout regularly rests on its jour-

Salmo trutta trutta—female

ney inland it is recognized as a traditional sporting fish. Artificial flies are popular when fishing for it, although in some places various natural and artificial baits are used. To a certain extent it is possible to compare the corresponding fishing techniques employed for the Brown Trout, for example the choice of flies, but the Sea Trout prefers gaily coloured flies, interwoven with an occasional silvery thread. Usually it is fished for with wet flies. Of these the traditional Butcher, Teal and Green, Silver March Brown, Cinnamon and Gold, Blue Kingfisher, Alexandra, Red Palmer, Black and Blue Zulu, and March Brown are the best. The angler usually manages with several basic types. When fishing for Sea Trout, it is advisable to change the size of flies rather than the types themselves. The fish lies indifferently on the bottom all day and activity only increases after nightfall when the search for food begins. When fishing in streams in the evening and at night, it is better to choose one fly only. On the wide open surface of the lake, up to three flies can be used. The bait must command the Trout's attention, attract it and excite it. Various phantoms, such as 'Demons' and 'Terrors' and in particular Teal and Solver, Alexandra and Jungle, Mallard and Blue can be successfully employed to do this. Fishing for Sea Trout at night can sometimes be remarkably rewarding, although the loss of flies can be great and therefore it is necessary to have a greater supply to hand than during the day. The flesh of the Sea Trout has an excellent taste and is similar to the flesh of all fishes of the Salmon family.

Salmo trutta trutta—detail of head

The Brown Trout

Salmo trutta fario

Salmon family

Salmonidae

The Brown Trout is well known for its beautiful appearance, the shape of its body and its coloration, and it is one of the most sought after fishes in the angling world. It is widely distributed over various parts of the world, after being introduced by fishing enthusiasts. As a result it is now resident in the whole of Europe, the Mediterranean, northern, central and southern Africa, Asia Minor, the U.S.A., New Zealand, South America and Japan. For example, Trout were imported into New Zealand from Scotland. They reverted to a migratory type, going to the sea and returning to the streams and rivers only to breed. The Brown Trout most often inhabits the fast-flowing streams of mountain and sub-mountainous regions and sometimes even the valleys. It can adapt its coloration to the changing conditions of its environment, so that even fishes caught in the same stream and the same place differ in colour. They are very sensitive to the amount of oxygen in the water, to the water temperature and certain concentrations of pollutants. They are usually found in the vicinity of supplies of clean water.

The Sea Trout is a close relative and in fact the ancestor of the Brown Trout which has inherited its elongated, torpedo-shaped body, enabling it to live in fast-flowing waters. The head, with its massive toothed jaws stretching far behind the eyes, shows that the fish can also feed as a predator. The lower jaw, which curves sharply upwards, is a typical feature of the males as in other members of the Salmon family. The curve of the caudal fin is noticeable in the young fishes,

Salmo trutta fario—male

The Brown Trout

continued

but disappears in the older ones. As with other members of the Salmon family, they have a skin fold between the dorsal and the caudal fin, called the soft dorsal fin.

In the upper reaches of rivers, Trout are the most commonly found fishes. Darker coloured smaller fishes are found in the cold rapid mountain streams, which flow over hard stony bottoms, down slopes, and through small woods. Trout which are 20 cm long, are considered fine sturdy specimens here. Trout can penetrate streams well above sea level (about 2,000 m), where they live alone as other species do not manage to get that far. Below the mountains, when the river begins to meander and undermines its banks, pools are formed where older and larger fishes weighing between 2 and 7 lb are found. Sometimes much heavier Trout can be caught. The weight and size of Trout, as with other species, depends on the nutritional value of the environment, so that it is common to find fishes of the same age but differing in size. Trout live to a relatively ripe old age. The discovery of a fish 49 years old has been recorded, living in a barren old well and only weighing 1 lb 13 oz. This is not typical as Trout in rich waters, such as ponds, grow considerably faster and to a greater size and weight.

The Brown Trout needs plenty of hideouts. It therefore likes rivers with large stones, overhanging banks, pools and weirs. If disturbed, it quickly disappears into its hideout, which it eventually leaves again. It often swims with its head against the current for better resistance and to see food passing

Salmo trutta fario—female

The Brown Trout

continued

by in the water. It does not thrive too well in controlled waters where it misses its hideaways and the plentiful supplies of suitable food adhering to large stones.

The Brown Trout can be found several years later in the same place; it only travels upstream to the river source in order to breed. Spawning takes place from the beginning of October until December. At this time Trout look around for the mouths of tributaries to find suitable spawning grounds. After spawning they return to their local habitat. The largest Brown Trout are often reminiscent in colour of the Sea Trout, particularly in the spawning season, when their silvery sheen is dominant. When the summer is warm and long, breeding is postponed to a later date. During the act of spawning, the female lays 1,000 to 1,500 large yellow eggs. The fry hatch from the spawn after many days. In natural conditions the spawn and the fry have many enemies and only a small number survive; losses can be as great as ninety-nine per cent. Therefore fishermen do not rely on natural spawning any more and deposit small Trout, brought up in artificial Trout hatcheries into streams and rivers.

After 3 years the fish reaches a length of 20 cm in a good environment and in exceptional circumstances may exceed this. The fry is not at first particular about the extent of its environment; it is satisfied with small streams, but as it grows its needs increase, above all in food resources. Large Trout are one of its enemies as cannibalism is common in the

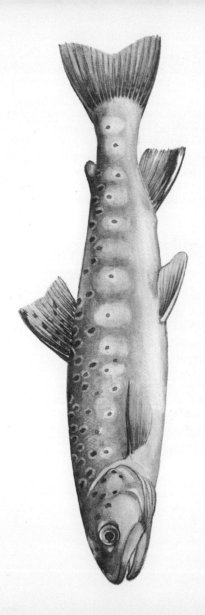

Salmo trutta fario—yearling with blue spots

The Brown Trout

continued

Trout species. At first Trout feed on small larvae, fresh-water shrimps and insects, which have sunk below the water surface; later they change over to predatory ways of feeding. Of all the fishes living in their waters they like the Lamprey, Minnow, Stone Loach and Gudgeon. If the Trout enters colder lakes, ponds, dams or flooded quarries, it can quite easily adapt to the new conditions. In such places it grows to an unusual size and yearly increases of 2 to 4 lb in large fishes are not rare, particularly in areas abounding with Minnows.

The Brown Trout living in deep waters usually stays most of the day at a great depth and it is difficult to reach it by the usual angling methods; it is best to fish for it by trailing a lure at depth behind a boat. The correct fishing season starts every year in spring. The main fishing methods are fly fishing and spinning. The most successful anglers often combine these two techniques depending on local conditions. When the angler is in the water wearing waders a crucial item of his tackle is a net, which enables him to land successfully even the largest Trout. The catch is often placed in a ventilated wicker-basket, slung round the angler's waist. When playing this fish a light rod with a small casting reel, a line of 5 lb breaking strain, and various types of small metal lures, usually spinners such as the Devon Minnow and others, are suitable. Various artificial fishes, and of course small plugs can be useful.

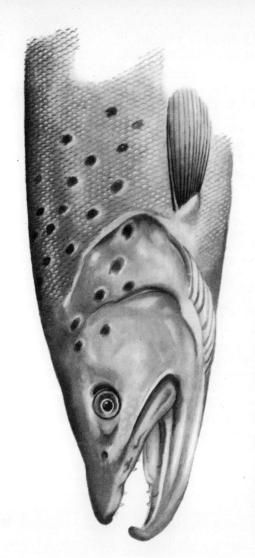

Salmo trutta fario—male, detail of head

The Brown Trout

continued

A detailed description of the elaborate scientific technique of fly fishing employed nowadays would require a separate book. It is enough to remind beginners and anglers only accustomed to the lower reaches of rivers that wet and dry flies are both possible and that such flies can be spun or allowed to flow freely. A wet fly is commonly used when fishing with the flow of the stream using a trace with one to three hooks. When using a dry fly, it is usual to have only one hook on the trace. When fishing cautiously so as to initially attract the fish, the line is usually cast downstream and the movements of the fly attract the fish. It is often necessary to dry out a dry fly and occasionally grease it.

To choose a suitable fly, it is advisable to have a look around the river banks and find out what insects are flying about on land and over the water. An examination of insects swimming in the water pays further dividends. For good results a knowledge of the habitats of large Trout is crucial, although fly fishing is difficult in extremely fast-flowing water. The angler should also know that the Trout is a shy fish and inhabiting clean water, it is able to see clearly above the surface. Therefore the angler should behave accordingly.

Those who have fished successfully for Trout, will find other types of fishing difficult to get used to, as fly fishing in fast currents of crystal clear water is definitely the most exhilarating form of the sport. In conclusion it is surely unnecessary to mention the excellent quality of Trout flesh.

Salmo trutta fario—adapted to life in still water

The Lake Trout

Salmo trutta lacustris

Salmon family

Salmonidae

Lake Trout have become domesticated in some Scottish, Alpine and Scandinavian lakes which have ice-cold and well-oxygenated water. Some anglers consider it a separate species, but in fact it is another form of the Sea Trout and the Brown Trout, although differing from them in coloration and body shape. The older fishes have a robust body with silvery sides and dark spots scattered over the head, dorsal or soft dorsal fin and extending below the lateral line. It inhabits very deep lakes, such as the Finnish Päijännen which is 104 m deep and where it lives solitarily or with other species of fish.

It breeds in autumn or at the beginning of winter on the gravelly, sandy beds of the lake's tributaries. Its offspring return to the lake after several years. In warm seasons it feeds on insect larvae and insects fallen into the water; in winter it lives predominantly on fishes, the Three-spined Stickleback in the north and even on small Perch. The females become sexually mature after the fourth year of life and grow more quickly than the males. Catches of 20 lb are not unknown.

The Brown Trout, which at times penetrates lakes and reservoirs, is inclined to change into Lake Trout in terms of body shape and coloration. After emptying the Yugoslavian reservoir, Lokvarka, Brown Trout were discovered weighing up to 50 lb. They had arrived as small fishes down the tributaries and their body shape in old age was not significantly different from the Lake Trout that man had put there.

The Lake Trout is caught by surface fly fishing or by various artificial metal lures. The largest specimens are caught by lures trailed at some depth behind a boat.

Salmo trutta lacustris—lake form

The Rainbow Trout

Salmo gairdneri

Salmon family

Salmonidae

The Rainbow Trout is typical of the waters of a vast area stretching from Southern Carolina to the south-east of Alaska, like the Brown Trout is a resident of European waters. It has developed a number of types in its native habitat. *Salmo gairdneri* is the original ancestor of all Rainbow Trout, although today it can be found on the American continent and many other places, for instance all over Canada, in the Great Lakes, in the states of New York and New England and along the shores of the Atlantic and Pacific Oceans. Once established in fresh waters, it usually remains there for all its life, but it is possible that during growth it may move to sea water for some time and then return to breed in fresh water later.

This fish species is ablaze with a wide range of colour from silver, black, violet, purple-red to green-blue. In descriptions of this fish in older literature many inaccuracies may be found which need correcting. A characteristic coloration of today's large Trout is often the purple-red stripe stretching from the head along the flanks to the tail. This is augmented by numerous small black spots scattered over the head, back and on the anal, caudal and dorsal fins. Usually the head is small while the body is covered with silvery scales that are forever gently flaking away. After 1881 the Rainbow Trout was imported from California to Germany and other countries because of its excellent rapid growth, but it only became domesticated in rivers and lakes in a few cases. According to data from the Alpine region, *Salmo trutta fario* and *Salmo gairdneri* compete mutually for food in its lakes and streams.

Salmo gairdneri—female from pond breeding

The Rainbow Trout

continued

Because of its resistance to higher water temperatures, its smaller oxygen requirement, and its ability to feed on different foodstuffs, the Rainbow Trout has become an exceptionally valuable fish species for artificial breeding purposes all over the world. Special, large capacity farms have been started, which produce yearly hundreds of tons of fishes for the consumer market.

This fish can be found in such special farms on all continents. It breeds during the spring months and, as the water gets warmer, incubation takes a shorter time. The fry, with a large yoke pouch attached, hatch out from the huge number of eggs after 1 to 2 months. According to its size one female usually lays up to 1000 eggs. The fry live at first on plankton and small larvae, later on larger crustaceans and small fishes. When artificially reared, they willingly accept blood or minced spleen and also granulated mixtures. In the first year they reach 10 to 15 cm in length according to living conditions and the availability of sufficient food and in the third year they reach 20 to 40 cm. Under favourable conditions they achieve a weight of 4 to 9 lb and in exceptional circumstances even more, especially in their homeland. They thrive in various types of still water without inflow or outlet, where they grow quickly in appropriate living conditions. Such suitable living conditions exist below dams where the cold lower layers of water have been released and which have the effect of equalizing temperature differences throughout the year. When smaller organisms are scarce, they sometimes start behaving as predators. Their ability to live in

Salmo gairdneri—male in the spawning season

The Rainbow Trout

continued

still waters has encouraged breeders in central Europe to
rear Trout in Carp ponds. Surprising results have been achieved in some flooded quarries, sand pits and old mine work-
ings, from which there was no possibility of the Trout escaping.

Fishing for Trout is very popular, and the Rainbow Trout
is always hungry and very voracious. It willingly rises to
artificial or natural baits all year round. In places where
winter fishing is possible, it may be caught on small lures
which can be dropped into holes in the ice. A hooked Trout
puts up a good fight and if it jumps above the water, it can
release itself from the hook and escape. Spinning is one of
the successful methods, which allows fishing to be carried
out in long stretches of the river and at different depths and
is best conducted from a boat in a reservoir. The type of
fly fishing is similar to that employed for the Brown Trout.
Artificial bait can differ in shape, size, colour combinations
and material. Small baits are the most common, for example
metal lures of about 5 cm long. A line of 7 lb breaking strain
is adequate; the length of the rod is chosen according to the
expanse of water and a light rod with a strong tip is best
of all. Wading is inevitable when fishing in flowing water.
Surface fishing is usually most successful towards evening in
places with a slow deep current, at the mouths of tributaries
or in lakes. During the day, fishing is more successful at
greater depths. The Rainbow Trout is not as good as the
Brown Trout as regards the quality of its flesh, but is its equal
as a sporting fish.

Salmo gairdneri—old male with a short firm body

The Charr
Salvelinus alpinus

Salmon family
Salmonidae

The Latin term for this fish indicates its connections with the Alps, but in fact it is not found in this area. It is a typical circumpolar species from the northern hemisphere, where it can be found off the shores of North America, Greenland, Iceland, Spitsbergen, Novaya Zemlya, the Bear Islands, Sweden, northern Norway and Siberia.

The jaws extend well behind the eyes and its beautifully coloured body is covered with small scales. While at sea, its back is metal blue, and its sides and belly are silvery. The sides are speckled with cream spots. In fresh water the coloration is generally lighter. The males are more brightly coloured, especially during spawning. The ventral fins are orange and the subsequent pair of fins, including the single anal fin, are reddish orange with a white lining. After several years living in fresh water the fishes return to the sea. They do not stray far from the mouth of their native river, as shown by the fact that marked individuals have been caught at a mere distance of 12 to 24 miles from the river estuary.

In the breeding season the return trip to fresh water starts in July and culminates in August, although migratory types spawn much later. According to her size, the female lays several thousand eggs. The speed of growth depends on how nourishing the environment is. The basic food consists of larvae, insects, worms and fishes such as the Stickleback. In Hudson Bay migratory Charr are to be found, which are as much as 50 cm long when 10 years old, in contrast to sedentary fishes which grow considerably more slowly. Fishes as old as 25 years have also been caught.

The Charr's flesh is very tasty and is often the staple diet of Eskimos and their dogs. Where it is found it has an economic value. Angling methods are similar to those used for other fishes of the Salmon family.

Salvelinus alpinus—male

The Alpine Charr

Salmon family

Salvelinus salvelinus

Salmonidae

This fish likes cold, high locations in the Alps, northern Norway, Ireland, Scotland and Iceland. It inhabits lakes situated at high altitude, about 2,000 m and above. Different types and varieties of this species often live in lakes not very far from each other.

The Alpine Charr is reminiscent of the Brown Trout in the shape of its body, but its coloration is different. The back is blue-green, the belly is yellow or a light orange-pink and small light yellow spots are to be seen on its sides and back. The vomerine bone is short, the scales are minute. All except the dorsal fin are lined with white on the lower side; a feature which is more noticeable in the males during the spawning season, when their belly turns deep red. Anglers have identified several forms in the Alpine lakes, which apart from other features differ in their breeding seasons; one form spawns in winter near the shore, another one in summer in deep waters. The largest predators reach a weight of 10 lb. Smaller fishes, living in deep water, feed on planktonic organisms and hardly grow to a length of 20 cm.

Angling techniques are similar to those used for other members of the Salmon family. When fishing in lakes, a boat is indispensable. These fishes can be caught by fly or by trailing artificial or natural bait. At dusk or at night they rise to the surface, and at such times fly fishing is usually most successful. The flesh is pleasantly flavoured, especially that of smaller fishes.

Salvelinus salvelinus—male

The Brook Trout

Salvelinus fontinalis

Salmon family

Salmonidae

This fish is justly classified as one of the most beautiful types of salmonid fishes. It comes from the eastern part of North America, from Manitoba, Ontario, Quebec, Newfoundland, Prince Edward Island, Nova Scotia, New Brunswick and the shores of Labrador. The Brook Trout was imported into Europe from America in about 1884, firstly into Germany and from there to other countries. According to the latest information it seems that the Brook Trout is leaving its native fresh waters and entering the sea as a result of qualitative changes in the environment, such as higher temperatures and the competition of other fishes. Migration and longer journeys usually begin at night.

The Brook Trout sets off for the sea in spring or at the beginning of summer; it leaves for the spawning grounds, upstream, in the second half of the year. It breeds in the same places and at the same time of the year (i. e. October, November) as *Salmo trutta*, with which it also easily crossbreeds. The crossbreds are beautifully coloured, with tiger stripes, but they are sterile. The female lays about 1,000 eggs per 1 lb of her weight. The fry hatch in several months, according to the water temperature. The Trout, which grow to the largest size, spend a part of their life at sea, where they feed on larvae and the fry of various fishes, such as the Stickleback, small Eel, Minnow, and various invertebrates. The freshwater Trout lives on the larvae of the Red Midge, Mayfly and Caddis Fly or on various worms, crustaceans, or insects which have fallen into the water and fish fry.

The fishes living at sea are a steely blue and green on their backs, silvery at the sides and completely white on the belly.

Salvelinus fontinalis—male

The Brook Trout

continued

The pink pectoral, ventral and anal fins are edged in brilliant white, whereas the caudal and dorsal fins are grey-green. During the journey from the sea to fresh water, guanine (fish silver) disappears from the basic colour tone and irregular stripes appear on the upper part of the body, stretching as far as the dorsal fin, changing into orange flecks on its sides and finally turning into red dots along the lateral line. When returning from the sea, the Trout is harassed by large parasitic crustaceans, until it sometimes dies from complete exhaustion.

The fishes, which live a part of their lives at sea, achieve a greater size as a result of better nourishment, for example 6 to 9 lb specimens are not rare. In contrast, fishes living in fresh water hardly reach 2 lb. The largest recorded specimen, caught in Nipigon in Ontario weighed 15 lb. In poor conditions they hardly reach 6 oz. From time to time they are transplanted into colder ponds, where they get on relatively well. In European waters they weigh about 1 to 2 lb and heavier fishes are rare.

The Brook Trout likes colder water, it does not require as many hideouts as the Brown Trout and it can survive in effectively controlled rivers. In comparison with another type bred in Europe, the Rainbow Trout, it is more stable and less of a wanderer. In its native habitat and locations it is considered a very valuable angling fish. Fishing for it in well-stocked still and flowing waters is a real pleasure. The flesh is exceptionally tasty and pink to red in colour, according to its lifelong diet. Fishing methods for the Brook Trout are the same as those used for other trout.

Salvelinus fontinalis—from waters of low nutritional value

The Huchen

Salmon family

Hucho hucho

Salmonidae

This fish is one of the most beautiful of large salmonid fishes inhabiting inland waters. Its head with jaws equipped with distinctive rows of teeth shows that it is a predator. The colour of the young Huchen is lighter than that of the older fish with its predominant green-brown colouring. In the spawning season the males are tinged pink at the sides and turn black on the belly. It is still possible to fish for Huchen in Czechoslovakia, Austria and Rumania, but as a result of the modernization of fishing techniques and increasing water pollution they are continually in decline. Experiments have been conducted in artificial rearing and the distribution of domesticated fishes to other parts of the world (for example they have been taken from Czechoslovakia to Algeria and Morocco). They live in deep streams where they find abundant food, such as Dace and Chub. They grow quickly and reach a weight of 40 lb and above. A fish caught was reported as weighing 110 lb. They breed in April or May.

Huchen are particularly sought after in autumn and in winter and fishing for them is very exacting. The habitat of Huchen is usually predictable and they search out their food early in the morning or early in the evening. They can be caught by spinning, and by using dead fishes, metal lures or plugs. Artificial animals are also good bait, such as common amphibians (for example the frog) or land vertebrates (for example the mouse). A large lure should be chosen with a line of 12 lb breaking strain and such a rod as will stand up to the sharp thrusts and the play of a large fish in flowing water. The Huchen's flesh is of a high quality and is excellent when smoked.

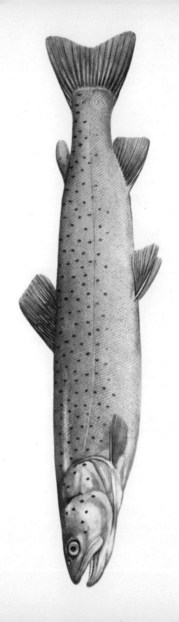

Hucho hucho—male

Coregonus albula

Whitefish family
Coregonidae

Coregonus albula belongs to the Whitefish (Coregonidae) family, but sometimes is classified as a member of the Salmon family, which is very inconsistent and at present there is regular and general confusion as to its representatives. *C. albula* has characteristic silvery, lightly flaking scales. In shape and coloration it resembles the Herring but it has the adipose fin characteristic of the Salmon family. It has typical gill filaments which are used as a filtration device.

C. albula lives predominantly in the lakes of northern Europe adjoining the shores of the Baltic Sea, from Denmark to Finland. It likes deep and clear water with gravelly, sandy bottoms, where it breeds between November and December. At this time the female lays about 30,000 eggs on the river bed. The fry and the adult fishes live on plankton. Attempts at domesticating the fishes in different types of water, for example in dams, have so far been only marginally successful.

It is very rare that *C. albula* is hooked in the process of fishing for other fishes. As a result of its plankton diet and its sensitive mouth this fish is not one which can be easily caught by the rod; it would require very sophisticated equipment, unlimited patience and also a detailed knowledge of the locality for any degree of success. In some lakes *C. albula* is found in abundance and then it can be caught in nets. It has a great market value and is usually preserved and tinned.

Coregonus albula

Freshwater Houting

Coregonus lavaretus

Whitefish family

Coregonidae

In its body shape and the arrangement and colour of its scales, this fish is similar to some lesser members of the Carp family. Its characteristic feature is its adipose dorsal fin. It originated in northern Europe from where it was exported to other places. Its habitat is the cold lakes of the north, which have very clear waters. Sometimes the larval fishes from hatcheries are put in Carp ponds where they thrive. It has even become domesticated and breeds naturally in some dams where it was experimentally planted. It lives in shoals.

Until the age of 3 years it lives predominantly on plankton, which it filters from the water with the help of its gill filaments. Later it also consumes invertebrates from the bottom, and the digestive organs of the largest specimens have also been found to contain fry. In favourable conditions it grows quickly and by the age of 3 or 4 years it can weigh 2 lb but usually does not exceed 4 lb. In warm weather it can be found in deeper places where the water is cold and well oxygenated, but at night it rises to the surface and visits the shallows. In November and December it comes into the shore, where it spawns on the gravel and sand.

Much time has been spent in discussing whether it is possible to catch this fish on a rod and line. The experience of recent years proves that if the timing is correct, that is at night and in the evening, and animal bait is used with a small hook and a line of 3 to 5 lb breaking strain, then rod fishing can be successful. On vast stretches of water they are best caught from a boat. Whether artificial or natural insect bait is used, a knowledge of fly fishing is useful for the occasion when the fishes rise to the surface. The flesh is very delicate and tasty and is most popular when roasted in butter or smoked.

118

Coregonus lavaretus

The Houting

Coregonus oxyrhynchus

Whitefish family

Coregonidae

The migratory Houting can be most often found in the coastal waters of the North Sea and the Atlantic Ocean and in adjacent rivers. The spawning grounds are located in the middle reaches of the rivers, where the fishes arrive at the end of summer. It is clear from historical records that it used to be a relatively frequent commodity at markets along the river Rhine, the Weser and the Elbe. As a result of increasing water pollution and the construction of weirs and dams it is becoming rare and now it does not enter some rivers at all. In Sweden it gets into lakes, where it often stays permanently and in places has developed into an exclusively freshwater type.

The Houting's body is robust and more thick-set than that of the Freshwater Houting. The crown of the head and the back are grey-green to a metal blue in colour, with silver shades becoming dominant towards the belly. On the head the mouth and the distinctive snout are in the inferior position and testify to the habitual search for food on the water bed where there is a plentiful supply of various larvae, worms and small molluscs. It therefore differs from other sedentary Charr, which live permanently in lakes and feed on plankton. The breeding season starts at the end of October and lasts until December. It spawns on hard, gravelly, sandy beds and the fry, as soon as they are hatched, are carried downstream to the sea. It is sometimes accidentally caught when fishing, but angling for it as such is not common. Incidentally if a large specimen is hooked, it can put up very effective resistance. The flesh is very tasty.

Coregonus oxyrhynchus

The Grayling

Thymallus thymallus

Grayling family

Thymallidae

The Grayling is justly ranked as one of the most beautiful freshwater fishes. It is noted for its large smooth scales, its adipose fin and a large dorsal fin, which is not possessed by any other fish inhabiting those parts of the river just below the mountains. The Grayling is splendidly coloured in the breeding season, the males being much gayer than the females. The dorsal fin is a dark red or violet with brown areas, whilst the gill covers are violet-blue. It is located in sub-mountainous zones of European rivers, except in southern France and Spain and there are related species living in Asia and North America. It reaches a weight of 1 lb, sometimes rising to 2 lb and lives to the age of 6 years. It breeds in spring on a sandy or gravelly bed. It stays in deep, running water near the bottom and rises to the surface for food. It mainly feeds on larvae and insects which have fallen into the water.

Great interest in fishing for it has led to it being artificially reared and deliberately located. Successful fishing for the Grayling is regarded as the zenith of the art of fishing. Peaceful autumn weather is necessary for good results, the best time being the period between 10 a.m. and 4 p.m. It requires sophisticated equipment (for example a rod with a fly fishing reel, and a quality line) and relatively small flies. It is caught on dry or wet flies. Wading into water improves the angler's performance and chances of success. Even larger specimens can be caught on small rotating metal lures, for example golden Devon Minnows in this context are good.

Its flesh is very tasty and has a distinctive spicy aroma.

Thymallus thymallus

The Pike

Esox lucius

Pike family

Esocidae

The Pike is the most popular predatory fish of inland waters. Its powerful teeth and wide-open mouth are reminiscent of a crocodile's head. Quick darts after prey are made possible by the rear location of its dorsal fin. Its teeth are renewed from time to time and their slanting position stops the prey escaping. The green shade of its body with yellowish dots is vital for lengthy stays in the aquatic undergrowth, where the Pike can find plenty of hideouts and food. Small Pike are slender and more colourful. The older fishes, especially the females, have robust bodies. The Pike is widespread in Europe, where it can be found not only in fresh water but also in brackish water off the coasts (apart from the southern ones). It also occurs in Asia, in the rivers flowing into Lake Aral, and in North America. It mainly lives a solitary existence and always in one spot; it frequents slow-running or still waters and rarely undertakes journeys outside its locality. Its length is usually about 1 m and its weight between 20 and 30 lb. In Siberia its upper weight limit is said to be 140 lb. It grows relatively quickly, larger Pike putting on weight faster than smaller ones whilst the females grow more quickly and live longer than the males.

The breeding season is in early spring from February to May, according to how warm it is. The female lays hundreds of thousands of eggs, according to its size, and deposits them on the recently flooded vegetation, close to the river banks. For sporting purposes in natural waters the breeding of Pike by natural means does not result in a sufficient number of

Esox lucius

The Pike

continued

fishes; Pike are therefore transplanted from the hatcheries as larval or several-month-old fishes, at which time they are 5 to 8 cm long. In places where dams have been constructed on 'Pike' rivers their number increases, as in the first few years after flooding such places provide excellent conditions for natural breeding on the freshly flooded vegetation. After several years, owing to the fluctuation in the water level and the consequent removal of vegetation from the banks, the natural Pike population rapidly declines. Because it grows quickly the Pike has even been located in places where it did not exist before, for example it thrives in Spain, where large increases in its length and weight have been recorded.

The larval Pike starts to look for food soon after hatching from the egg; at first it eats plankton, later the fry of other fishes and even those of its own close relatives are not spared. If there are Perch and Roach in the Pike's neighbourhood, these always constitute the largest part of its diet, some fifty to seventy per cent, in fact. It is known that for a 2 lb increase in weight Pike eat 8 to 12 lb of smaller, insignificant types of fishes. Feeding does not stop in winter; on the contrary valuable types of fish begin to form a large portion of its food. The Pike therefore is not a welcome resident of Trout lakes and streams, as it can destroy large numbers of Trout and Charr. It often attacks prey which are only a little smaller than itself and it is not unknown for two Pike of similar size to be found, one trying to eat the other.

The Pike presents the angler with many possibilities for

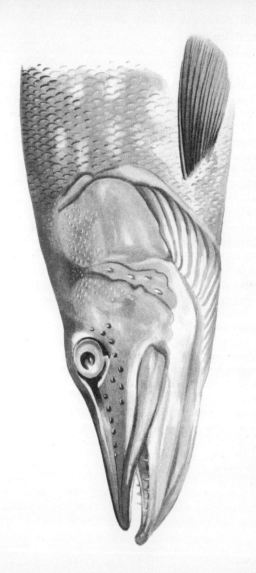

Esox lucius—detail of head

The Pike

continued

interesting fishing. Peaceful autumn weather and the early hours of the morning are the best time for it. In autumn when its sex glands start producing new secretions, the Pike becomes very voracious, the female more so than the male. In Canada, the U.S.A., Finland and other countries it is customary to fish for it in winter, under the midday sun and on the frozen surface of large rivers and lakes. Fishing with live fishes (for example Crucian Carp, Perch, Gudgeon and Roach) is most common, in which case a long rod with a strong tip section is most useful and the shallows near the banks are the best location. A large float is essential to hold the live bait near the water surface. The hook is at the end of a wire trace to prevent the pike biting through the line. After the bait is taken, line is released and when it stops and is then taken again the hook is firmly embedded. Fishing with spinners and plugs definitely shows the most sportsmanship. When using this method, the venue is changed and the Pike has to be searched for. When trailing with a suitable spinning rod, a casting reel with a sufficient length of line of 7 to 9 lb breaking strain and of course a wire trace are used. In dense undergrowth plugs are often successful if worked along the water surface. The fish is finally landed by a large net or gaff.

Opinions as to the taste and quality of the Pike's flesh vary. It cannot be compared with the flesh of Salmon, but when suitably prepared, it can make a very tasty dish. It is not eaten in some places (for example England and Scotland), but this fact does not diminish its reputation there as a sporting fish.

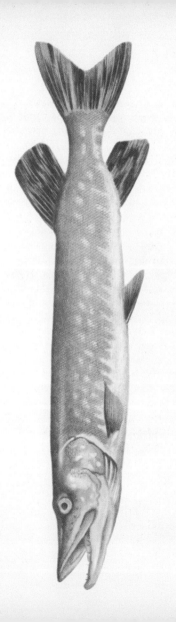

Esox lucius—yearling of different colour and body structure

The Roach

Rutilus rutilus

Carp family

Cyprinidae

The Roach is widespread throughout Europe, except for the region south of the Alps, and is one of the most numerous fishes in slow-flowing or still, muddy waters. Its confusion with the Rudd is easily eliminated as the Roach's dorsal fin is situated in front of the ventral fins, the iris is deep red and the ventral, anal and caudal fins are yellow to light red. The mouth is relatively small and is centrally situated, whilst its pharyngeal teeth are in a single row. In some land-locked waters without predators it can multiply so fast that its growth becomes stunted and at the same time intensifies the competition with other more valuable species in the quest for food. It usually reaches a length of 20 to 30 cm, weighs barely 1 lb, rising to 2 lb in exceptional cases, and lives for up to 15 years.

Breeding takes place from the end of April to the beginning of May depending on the water temperature. The female lays spawn on water-covered plants and the roots of trees. In old dams without a layer of vegetation it even spawns on the rock base or gravel deposits near the shore. According to her size the female sheds several thousand pink eggs, about 1 mm in size. When breeding, it gathers in large shoals so that the spawning grounds are usually covered with whole 'carpets' of spawn. Initially the Roach lives on plankton, but later graduates to insect larvae and insects swimming on the surface.

From an angling standpoint it is a very significant and

Rutilus rutilus—male with spawning rash

highly prized fish in various club competitions. It very nearly has a perpetual appetite and so it can be caught nearly all the year round, within, of course, limits specified by local regulations. It is possible to catch it even when the water is frozen. Groundbait is always very helpful and the best is made from bread crumbs or wet bread. In cold weather, bait such as maggots or worms is more effective, while in summer bait such as bread paste or hemp seed is better.

It pays dividends to change the bait. For best results, hollow glass or cane rods with a fine tip, a very thin line of about 1 lb breaking strain, and a small float are used. The hook is very fine and the float always very small and sensitive. Real experts in the field fish for Roach with only one rod and try to keep the bait moving all the time. Baiting, hooking, reeling in and rebaiting are carried out with a regular, almost monotonous rhythm. It is possible to buy bait pastes with additional ingredients in angling shops. Anglers have developed their own secrets of how to prepare colourful and scented pastes. Today the Roach is a fish which has forced anglers to develop sophisticated techniques as no other species before. In eastern and north-eastern Europe it is one of the most popular angling fishes and is even caught under the ice.

The flesh has a high content of intermuscular bones, but sometimes is processed and tinned.

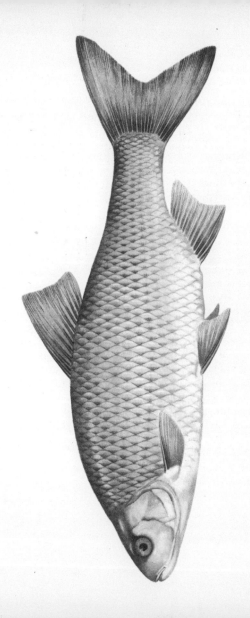

Rutilus rutilus—from a mountain stream

The Chub

Leuciscus cephalus

Carp family

Cyprinidae

This fish is found mainly in running waters throughout Europe with the exception of northern Scotland, Ireland and Denmark. It also likes to enter still waters, which are temporarily joined to a river or a stream. It inhabits all the fish habitats but is most numerous in waters characterized by the presence of Barbel. It has a broad head with a large mouth and it can be distinguished from Dace by its rounded anal fin. Its large scales with a silvery sheen are edged in black, whilst the anal and ventral fins are a deep red. It is not particular about the quality of the water and can be found even in municipal waste water, at the openings of sewers etc.

It eats almost everything from algae, bits of vegetation, and various seeds that have fallen into the water, to insects and their larvae and worms. It can even swallow a small frog or a drowned mouse and also catches prey from among the shoals of small fishes. Its usual weight is about 1 lb, but sometimes it is heavier, rising to 4 lb at a length of about 50 cm and in rare cases even up to 8 lb. It grows slowly and by the age of 6 years it only weighs about 8 oz and is 25 cm long. It matures sexually in the third or fourth year of its life. It breeds at the end of spring on the gravelly river bottom in midstream. The males exhibit at this time a spawning rash in the form of white hard growths on their heads. The female lays 20,000 to 100,000 eggs. Chub grow more quickly in dams than in flowing water, especially the larger specimens which change to a predatory existence.

The Chub is popular among anglers for its general voracity which sets no limits on the choice of fishing techniques. It is

Leuciscus cephalus—river form

possible to fish successfully for it all year round, even in winter. Sometimes it requires considerable skill as it is quite often very shy, moody and particular as regards food. Large fishes are most difficult to catch. In winter animal bait is commonly used, including small fishes, such as Minnows, which are hooked by the lip or near the head. Even stuffed intestines of poultry and maggots have turned out to be successful bait. The tackle should be sensitive, but firm and the bait should crawl along the water bottom. It is possible to fish with success using cherries, morellos, plums, raspberries, blackberries, boiled peas or tomatoes. Even stewed fruit is effective but fastening it to the hook proves difficult. When fishing for large fishes, the line is left fairly slack as the bite can be a very strong one and the angler must have plenty of time to react and hook the fish.

Fishing by vibrating live or dead insect bait is an interesting angling technique. It is most often effective when the angler can hide on the river bank among the trees, whose branches reach out over the water. When using this method, very fine, long rods with springy tips and fine lines are employed. The effect on the water surface is achieved by a finger knocking on the rod; this vibration is transmitted along the rod to its tip, down the vertical line and so to the bait. Bait used for this purpose includes butterflies, cockchafers, grasshoppers and flies. Artificial wet or dry flies are similarly helpful.

Chub flesh is not very tasty, especially that of fishes living in polluted waters.

Leuciscus cephalus—lake form

The Dace

Leuciscus leuciscus

Carp family

Cyprinidae

This fish can be readily distinguished from Chub by its curved anal fin, that of the Chub being rounded. The body is more elongated and covered with larger scales, which have not the dark lining of those of the Chub. Black-blue with a metallic sheen is the basic colour shade of its back. All the fins, except the dorsal which is usually darker, are yellow or orange.

In Europe, except for Ireland, Scotland and southern countries, it can often be found in the vicinity of Trout, but more commonly in the vicinity of Grayling. It can even be numerous in Barbel waters. In lakes, with adjacent streams, its body has a deeper form. It does not normally assume large proportions, the largest specimens being 30 cm long and weighing about 11 to 14 oz, and rarely more than this. Small Dace search for food in shoals whereas large Dace swim about briskly by themselves just under the surface and collect the insects which have fallen from the banks and trees into the water. In Trout and Grayling waters Dace are not welcome in large numbers, as they compete with those fishes for food.

It is possible to catch Dace using natural insects and using the same vibration technique as employed for Chub. In densely populated waters it can be caught by surface fishing with artificial flies. The flesh is not highly prized as it is too dry and contains a number of intermuscular bones. Dace therefore does not have any economic significance, but is appreciated by skilled anglers.

Leuciscus leuciscus

The Orfe

Carp family

Leuciscus idus

Cyprinidae

This fish differs from other Dace-like fishes in its small scales and small mouth. The pectoral, ventral and anal fins are red. The back is a dark green-blue, while the sides shimmer with a silver sheen. It can be found in European waters except British ones, starting at the Rhine and extending as far as the large rivers of Siberia. It likes lowland rivers and frequents their little creeks and coves. It has been experimentally reared with success in ponds, where its body is deeper. It is very sensitive to pollution and rigid control of the river banks. In favourable conditions it can weigh several pounds, but its usual weight is 1 to 2 lb with a length of 40 cm.

The Orfe usually lives in shoals and feeds on stray insects. In autumn when the water becomes colder, it moves down to a greater depth. It breeds in spring, when the female lays several thousand eggs. Both sexes in the breeding season acquire a golden coloration and the males develop a spawning rash. Rearing the golden form in ornamental ponds is a popular pastime.

Angling for Orfe is very popular and it is possible to catch them on literally any bait. They can be caught on artificial flies and small metal lures. The largest Orfe have been caught by trailing dead or live fishes such as Minnows. Once hooked the Orfe resists ferociously and playing it is therefore a real delight. Shoals of Orfe can be discovered near natural hideaways, under weirs and overhanging banks. It is also possible to entice and catch them with boiled sweet corn, peas and dough. It frequently happens that they take bait prepared for Carp. The Orfe's flesh is relatively tasty and is very popular in places where the fish abounds.

Leuciscus idus

Alburnoides bipunctatus

Alburnoides bipunctatus penetrates further up river than a similar fish, the Bleak. It is commonly found with Trout, in tranquil places such as pools and above weirs, and usually in the company of Minnows. Its body is laterally flatter but deeper than the Bleak's, and the mouth position is central rather than on top. The eyes are large and the fin roots are pink. The predominant colour is dark silver. The lateral line bends behind the head and is accompanied along its whole length by dark stripes. This fish does not exceed 10 cm in length and only rarely lives to an age of 6 years. It is not found in the northern or southern countries of Europe, nor in England or Ireland.

Anglers often are not aware of its presence in the river; it never multiplies so fast that it outnumbers other species. It breeds in May, when the female lays several thousand eggs in the peaceful, slow-moving stretches of the river. It lives on various small aquatic organisms, such as insect larvae and dead insects.

A. bipunctatus has no economic importance but forms the prey of predatory fishes. As such it is useful as live bait when fishing for predators. It is most likely to be caught in inlets, pools and places with a slow current, on a small hook with the thinnest line and by float fishing.

Alburnoides bipunctatus

The Minnow

Phoxinus phoxinus

Carp family
Cyprinidae

The Minnow inhabits cold, running or still, yet well oxygenated, waters throughout Europe. It can be found in those parts of streams where the water current is sluggish and leaves deposits of fine mud and sand. It lives in small or large groups according to the extent of its environment and quite often in the company of *Alburnoides bipunctatus* or the Stone Loach. In body shape it is ranked with those slim fishes which have an elongated body and long tail-ends. Its scales are only numerous on its sides. Its back is an olive-green shade and from there a row of transverse flecks of differing length spread down its body.

During breeding in May, it is easy to distinguish the male from the female. The male's coloration at this time is much brighter; it has a white spawning rash on its head which resembles semolina, whilst the belly, pectoral and ventral fins turn a blood red and the olive-green of the back changes to black. The female's sides and belly are a mixture of grey-brown tones and the red colour is missing; the belly is considerably enlarged before spawning.

The Minnow does not reach a large size or an old age in any of its localities. It measures 10 to 12 cm and does not live longer than 4 to 5 years. Sometimes it is deliberately put into Trout waters, especially lakes and larger streams, because it is the staple food of large Trout. If it enters a pond, it can multiply very quickly. Anglers consider it excellent bait when fishing for members of the Salmon family. They catch it in small nets and also with small hooks using various insects or small pieces of worm.

Phoxinus phoxinus—male (above) and female (below), distinguished by colouring

The Rudd

Scardinius erythrophthalmus

Carp family

Cyprinidae

This fish is very similar to the Roach. It can be easily recognized by the rear position of its dorsal fin, its deep red fins, as opposed to the Roach's yellow ones and its yellow and orange iris, as opposed to the Roach's crimson one. Its pharyngeal teeth make up two rows and its mouth is turned upwards, whereas the Roach's mouth is in the central position. The silvery sheen of the large scales on its sides changes, as the fish grows older, into a golden yellow shade.

The Rudd can be found over most of Europe in sunny and slow-flowing or still, lowland waters, where it can find suitable plant food. It usually stays near the surface on sunny days but when it is cloudy it remains near the bottom. It spawns in spring on flooded vegetation, where the female lays several thousand eggs. Once it reaches river ponds or overgrown reservoirs it spreads quickly. The largest Rudd can weigh over 2 lb, but fishes weighing 1 lb are considered good specimens. In Scandinavian waters they have lived to 19 years.

Fishing for Rudd allows a wide range of choice in terms of fishing methods and baits. Similar techniques as those used for Roach can be employed if fine equipment is used. When using a float, the depth of the hook is set at about half that of the water, although fishing near the surface can also be rewarding. If no other bait is available, a bit of alga or a piece of lettuce will do. During hot summer days, towards evening, fly fishing with artificial or natural insects is possible and quite often a favourable response is obtained by tapping the rod. Rudd provides good bait when fishing for predators, especially Pike.

Scardinius erythrophthalmus

The Asp

Carp family

Aspius aspius

Cyprinidae

This is the only predatory species of the Carp family. Its symmetrical body shows it to be a good swimmer. The large caudal fin with its deep curve enables the fish to launch sudden attacks on its prey. The mouth is wide, with the lower jaw protruding upwards over the top one. Both jaws are toothless but have very hard lips, which resist the hook. Small Asp are similar in appearance to Bleak for which they can be easily mistaken.

Asp live in the lower reaches of the river, in Barbel and Bream waters. They like to stay near bridge pillars, near tributaries, under weirs, in deep currents and overgrown parts of the river and in quiet bays of the river bends. They give away their presence to anglers by sudden attacks on prey near the water surface, especially on shoals of Bleak. This swift attack is reminiscent of an oar splashing the water with its flat side. In European waters, except for Denmark, France, Great Britain, Switzerland and southern regions, the Asp is more numerous than the angler's haul would suggest.

Breeding takes place in spring, in shallow, running water. The female, depending on her size, lays 50,000 to 400,000 eggs on gravel. This is the only time Asp gather in shoals; otherwise they live a solitary existence, although young fishes in twos to fives like to swim near the surface during sunny days. They grow relatively quickly and at the age of three are 30 to 47 cm long. In a suitable environment they can weigh 18 to 22 lb and in exceptional cases even more.

The Asp is a very valuable sporting fish as it is not easy to outwit. It is very shy and if the angler does not become

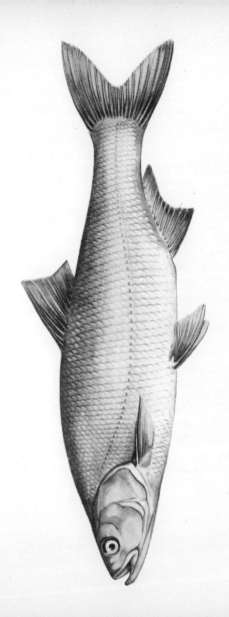

Aspius aspius

perfectly acquainted with its pattern of life and its behaviour in certain stretches of the river, he is not likely to be able to boast a good catch. Only occasionally will it react to ordinary types of bait. In slow-flowing water spinning is effective, using spoons supplemented by a red fringe on three hooks. A silver spoon up to 5 cm long is suitable for fishing in midstream. The line should be thin, about 7 lb breaking strain, and without a wire trace. The line is always cast several metres further away from the spot where the fish first revealed itself by its sudden surface movement. The lure is then retrieved only a few centimetres below the surface. When hooked, the Asp frenziedly tries to escape and so the check on the reel must be released. It is advisable to frequently change the type of lure being used.

Dead fishes, such as Bleak (if hooked at the side), trailed along the surface can prove effective. Live Bleak on a small hook and a thin line unimpeded by weights and other supplementary devices have also been employed with success, if left to mingle freely with a shoal of its companions near the surface. When the Asp attacks, the shoal quickly disperses, leaving only the bait, but the Asp and sometimes other predators do not usually leave it alone very long. Favourable times for fishing are early in the evening, at sunset, or in river currents all day long. Surprising results have been achieved when fishing with small or large artificial flies of light colour, white proving best of all. An Asp caught on a fly rod fights vigorously and its stout defence is comparable to that of members of the Salmon family.

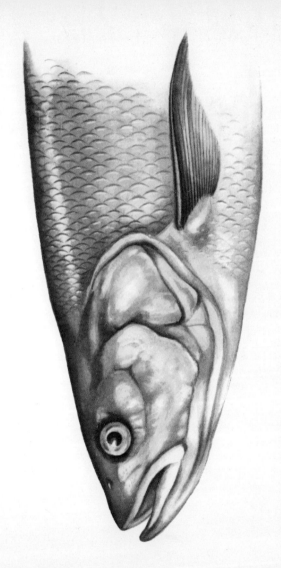

Aspius aspius—detail of head

The Tench

Tinca tinca

Carp family

Cyprinidae

The Tench is an important sporting fish, belonging to the Carp family. The body has the characteristic cylindrical shape and is covered by elliptical scales, the greater part of which are firmly embedded in the thick mucus-coated skin. At the corners of its fleshy mouth there are two small barbels. The most common basic coloration is dark green, brown-black and sometimes a golden shade is predominant, but usually all these are blended together. At present it lives almost all over Europe, from where it has been exported to fresh places. It inhabits still or slow-running waters which have warm inlets with an abundance of aquatic vegetation and muddy bottoms. The Tench has been introduced to and has settled down in colder waters, such as those of the Alps up to a height of 1,600 m above sea level or in peat-bog lakes with acid waters. The Tench is a traditional pond fish in central Europe, where it is reared with Carp or on its own.

The Tench breeds in the second half of June or in July and the larval Tench barely weigh 0.2 oz at the end of the first year, although by that time they can be sexually differentiated. This distinction is, however, easier with older fishes than younger ones. The males have thick fin rays and enlarged ventral fins, which often reach behind the anal passage, in contrast to those of the females, which are narrower, shorter and do not reach that far. Their growth is slower in poor waters situated high above sea level than in the rich waters of the lowlands. Experience of pond rearing has shown that the females grow faster than the males. In some waters the Tench grows to a weight of 6 to 9 lb, but

Tinca tinca

this is unusual and a 2 lb fish is regarded as a fine specimen.

It is a well-known fact among anglers that the Tench plays with the bait for a long time and this is best illustrated by float fishing, when the float starts dancing about. It is not therefore advisable to be too hasty in hooking this fish. It is best to fish for it before breeding starts, when the Tench is busy looking around for food and moves about in shoals, since at such times one can expect several fishes to bite in quick succession. These fishes bite best early in the morning and in the evening before dusk. They reveal their presence by the gentle waving movements of water plants and the subsequent rising of bubbles, released from the bottom. The best bait is white maggots or worms fished near the bottom or close to it, but bread paste and potatoes are also effective. It likes to eat freshwater molluscs and therefore thrives well in warm river ponds and muddy waters, where such organisms are relatively plentiful. After hooking, the fish should be steered away from the undergrowth and bushes, as it always tries to hide in them. Tench can survive for several hours when carried on dry land if wrapped in a damp tea-cloth. In older fishing journals it was often argued that predators, especially Pike, never attack Tench, but I have seen a Pike caught by using a Tench.

The Tench is a very popular market fish in West Germany and Italy where the taste of its flesh is compared with that of the Rainbow Trout. The flesh is generally considered very tasty, especially that of smaller fishes. The flesh, with the exception of large pieces, is not skinned in preparation, nor are the scales scraped off as they dissolve when fried.

Tinca tinca—from peat-bog lake

The Gudgeon

Gobio gobio

Carp family

Cyprinidae

The Gudgeon is one of those well-known fishes which have a variety of local names. It is small, scarcely growing to a length of 15 cm or reaching a weight of 10 oz, and only lives about 5 years. In shape it is similar to small Barbel in some ways. The body is covered with lightly flaking scales and has a silvery or bluish sheen. It has two barbels at the corners of its fleshy mouth. It can be found throughout Europe except in the most northerly and southerly parts. It is even located in brackish waters, sometimes in large shoals.

This fish lives in swiftly flowing water as well as in ponds, where it multiplies quickly. It usually moves about in shoals in those places where it is numerous and likes to hide on the sandy bottom behind scattered stones. It prefers places with a hard bed. It may even be found in comparatively polluted waters.

The Gudgeon is an excellent bait fish and is one of the most popular and best known types among anglers. As live bait below a float, it moves about with unusual liveliness and attracts the predator with its persistent darting movements towards the river bed. If it is fished at the bottom near stones or pieces of wood, it likes to hide behind them or often lies dormant. After rain it likes to enter clouded water in its search for food. Anglers sometimes make the water artificially cloudy with the help of a turf and then catch Gudgeon in it by float fishing, using the smallest hook with pieces of worms, various maggots and other bait. Although in size it is small, its flesh has an excellent flavour and therefore it is appreciated by gourmets in many places, such as France.

Gobio gobio

The Nase

Carp family

Chondrostoma nasus

Cyprinidae

This fish is one of the group that lives on plants and is found in small numbers in the waters of central Europe. It lives on the algal growths on stones, which are scraped away by its sharp, low, slit-like mouth. It moves in large shoals against the current and when the shoal turns aside after food it attracts attention by the glint of the many bodies. One fish can eat 32,000,000 to 96,000,000 microscopic algae, called diatoms, in a day. This fish can be found in the rivers which flow into the North and Baltic Seas and in the watershed of the river Danube. It is one of the most numerous fish species in certain parts of some rivers and can constitute more than fifty per cent of the fish population in such places.

The spawning season starts at the end of April, when large numbers of fishes concentrate in small areas. The females deposit about 20,000 light ochre eggs on to the stony or sandy bed. When adult, the fishes weigh about 2 lb, but rarely more.

Float fishing for them, although it makes demands on anglers and their equipment, is great sport. The bait is fished about 10 cm above the bottom of the river. Only an experienced angler can tell if the float has disappeared under the surface because a fish has bitten or because the hook has caught behind a stone or a root. Boiled barley, insect larvae or small maggots make appropriate bait and a feed os groundbait while fishing keeps the shoal within the angler's reach. The flesh is tasty but relatively greasy. A black membrane in the ventral cavity typifies this species, but it can easily be removed and does not influence the taste in any way.

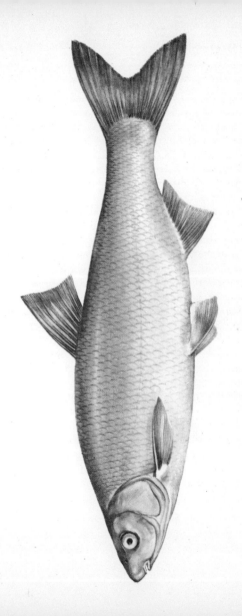

Chondrostoma nasus

The Bitterling

Carp family

Rhodeus sericeus amarus

Cyprinidae

The Bitterling is a small fish which reaches a length of barely 8 cm. It is known to aquarists more than anglers, despite it being relatively numerous, especially in Europe. It is only missing from the fringe areas of Europe, in the north (Scandinavia), in the south (Spain and Italy) and in the west (Britain and Ireland). It has been introduced by aquarists to various other places. It usually lives for 4 or a maximum of 5 years.

The males are larger than the females, which is unusual among fishes, and they are beautifully coloured in the spawning season. As well as the usual green-blue stripe on the sides at the back, the dorsal and anal fins become reddish and lined with black, the sides become silvery pink and the back turns dark blue. White tubercles appear on the snout. Spawning occurs in clear, slow-running or still water, often with a muddy bottom, and the presence of nearby fresh-water mussels is of vital importance. Just before spawning, the female grows an ovipositor by means of which she inserts her eggs within the valves of the mussel. The male sheds sperm into the inhalent current of the respiring mussel and thus fertilizes the eggs. After several days the fry hatch out and remain in the mussel until no longer requiring protection. The Bitterling repays its debt to the mussel in a similar manner, since the mussel larva spends some time of its development attached to a Bitterling.

Anglers do not like to use Bitterling as bait. Its flesh is supposed to be bitter and rejected by predators, although it has been found in their digestive organs.

Rhodeus sericeus amarus—male (above)
and female (below) in the spawning season

The Bleak

Alburnus alburnus

Carp family

Cyprinidae

This fish is well known to anglers as an excellent bait fish. It never grows very large, usually up to 15 cm and seldom up to 20 cm. It does not live longer than 6 years. It only grows quickly in the first year of its life, when it reaches 6 to 10 cm. In some ways it is similar to small Asp for which it can be mistaken as regards body shape and its silvery coloration. It has large eyes and a mouth in an upper position. It lives almost everywhere in Europe, except in Scotland and Ireland.

Bleak travel about in shoals near the surface in the zone where Barbel are found, but more often in the zone where Bream are found. Sometimes large groups like to stay in places into which various sewers open. It feeds largely on plankton, but it also likes to eat insects.

The Bleak provides excellent bait for all predators, whether dead and fished near the bottom for Pike and Perch or alive and swimming near the surface. It is best caught on small hooks with a baited fly, but can also be caught on a small artificial dry fly. Care must be taken, as its muscles are very soft and it can wriggle off the hook easily.

The flesh is very ordinary, but has been successfully preserved in oil like sardines.

Bleak used to be known for the fact, that the silvery pigment from its scales called 'Essence d'Orient' was used in the manufacture of artificial pearls. It takes about 4,000 Bleak to produce 4 oz of this essence.

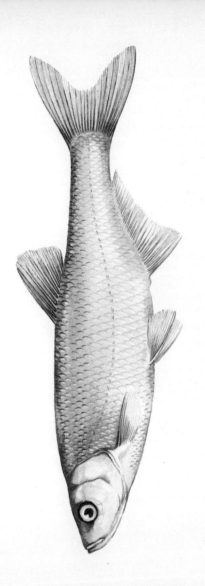

Alburnus alburnus

The Barbel

Barbus barbus

Carp family
Cyprinidae

This fish inhabits small and large European rivers, except for those in Scandinavia, Ireland, Denmark and the southern peninsulas. It is distinguished by its regular body shape and the symmetrical arrangement of its rows of scales. The flattened lower part of its body and fleshy mouth with four barbels indicate that it stays near the bottom in its search for suitable food.

The Barbel spends its time in deep currents. It uses its snout on the hard gravel or stony bed to turn over small stones and collect from them various insects and larvae. It is a slow-growing fish; for instance a 63 cm long Barbel, weighing 4 lb 11 oz was 18 years old. However, its weight is relative to the nutritional value of its environment. It can weigh 18 lb or more, but today such a fish is a rarity. With the current rate of water pollution, dam and weir construction, and river control the number of Barbel is fast decreasing. The spawning season is in June, when the eggs are deposited in the shallows and adhere to various kinds of bed. Before spawning a migration occurs, the fishes moving slowly upstream in large shoals.

It is a great experience to hook a fine Barbel, since when this happens the angler has to prove his efficiency and the quality of his equipment. The fish fights strongly in deep currents so that it seems as if the hook has caught under a stone or a sunken piece of wood. Large firm Carp hooks are usually selected, with a line of 12 lb or more breaking strain. This corresponds to that used with a Carp rod. It is possible to fish for it using ledgering or float-fishing techniques. Suitable baits are worms, Caddis Fly larvae, cheese, bread paste and small, whole, or pieces of dead fishes. The quality of its flesh is ruined by the prevalence of intermuscular bones.

Barbus barbus

The Silver Bream

Blicca bjoerkna

Carp family
Cyprinidae

The Silver Bream is a common resident of still and sluggish waters over almost all Europe. In appearance it is similar to the Bream, with which it is often confused. It is, however, smaller in size and has a smaller number of rays in its dorsal and anal fins and a smaller number of scales along the lateral line. The body is covered by large, regular scales with a silvery bronze coloration. The pectoral and ventral fins are reddish. There are two rows of pharyngeal teeth.

In some places, for example the river Elbe, it can breed profusely and adversely influence the growth of fishes with which it competes for food. Its food consists of crustaceans, insects and plants. The Silver Bream reaches a length of up to 20 cm, but fishes of 8 to 10 cm long are sexually mature and able to breed. The female lays her eggs in May and June on the roots of alder or willow trees or among any water plants. This fish forms a part of the predatory fish's diet and provides anglers with a bait fish.

Anglers who like to fish with extra-fine equipment will enjoy catching Silver Bream. They are relatively voracious and in some places it is possible to fish for them all year round. They can be caught by ledgering as well as by float fishing. The latter method is employed when fishing at a depth of up to 2 m in reeds and among other water plants. In such a case the rod is always as long as possible, with a line of 3 lb breaking strain, and very fine hooks. The bait can be varied according to the situation and the food that the fish has grown used to in its particular environment. When using paste, only the tip of the hook is hidden in it and during fishing, groundbait is scattered. The Bream is not really suitable for eating, as it has a great number of membrane bones. Nevertheless when fried in oil it is very popular in some places.

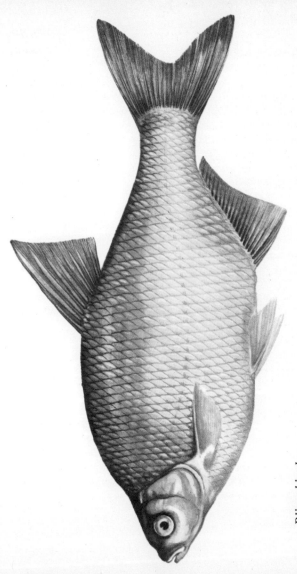

Blicca bjoerkna

The Bream

Abramis brama

Carp family

Cyprinidae

This fish can be found everywhere in Europe with the exception of the southern peninsulas. It is characterized by its body shape, which is deep and laterally compressed. The fish is bronze in colour and it has a relatively small head. Its puckered mouth indicates that it collects its food off the bottom, and the shape of its body suggests that it tends to stay at a great depth. When looking for food it swims at an angle. On average it weighs 1 to 4 lb, but even 15 lb specimens have been caught.

The Bream frequents still and slow-running waters where it travels about in large shoals. It likes dams, where it breeds to such an extent that it has to compete for food with other fish species. When overbreeding occurs growth becomes stunted. The Bream spawns at the end of May and at the beginning of June on to flooded grass or the roots of trees. The females mature sexually 3 or 4 years later than the males and they also live longer. During breeding, the males have a white rash on their heads.

The Bream is relatively highly valued by anglers. Fine equipment is necessary when fishing for it and such tackle should include a line of 5 lb breaking strain, a long fine rod and light but sharp hooks. The Bream looks for food all year round but with special intensity in the autumn. It is usually fished with the float lying flat on the water and with a taut line, and it is hooked straight after it bites. It can also be caught from a boat, when short, so-called boat rods are used. Effective baits include various larvae and maggots, boiled barley, sweet corn, peas, potatoes and various bread pastes. The flesh is greasy and contains many bones but can be smoked or used for making delicious soup.

Abramis brama

Abramis ballerus

Carp family
Cyprinidae

Although *Abramis ballerus* is similar to the Bream, it can be easily distinguished from it. For example its mouth is in a superior rather than inferior position, it has a lower and more elongated body with a longer anal fin, and there are a greater number of scales along its lateral line. It can be found in quiet waters in central and eastern Europe, in the watersheds of the rivers Danube and Volga, where in certain places it appears in large numbers. If dams are constructed on the river, it can adjust itself to the change from running to still water.

Unlike the Bream it feeds mainly on planktonic organisms. It does not achieve large proportions and usually grows to between 20 and 30 cm. It breeds in spring, when the female lays her eggs on submerged plants or the gravelly bottom. The males grow faster than the females and reach a weight of up to 2 lb. These fishes commonly live until the age of 10 years but even 17 year old fishes have been caught.

Salted or dried, this fish is a delicacy eaten in eastern Europe with beer or vodka, but it has not acquired any economic importance in such places.

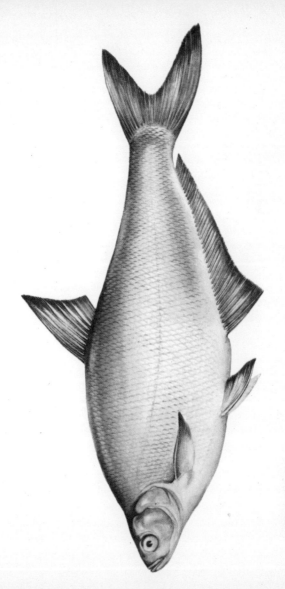

Abramis ballerus

Vimba vimba

Carp family
Cyprinidae

This fish has a wide ventral mouth with fleshy lips. A spindle-shaped body suggests a tendency to swim in strong currents. The grey-blue to brown-green coloration on the back and the silvery sides change in the spawning season. The back becomes darker and turns to black and an orange stripe appears along the underside of the body, while the roots of its fins take on an orange sheen. The males have a spawning rash on their head in the form of whitish nodules. The young fishes can be mistaken for *Chondrostoma nasus*.

Vimba vimba is one of the inhabitants of the rivers that run into the Baltic Sea, and it also lives in the river network of the Danube, but in a slightly different form. In the 6 to 8 years of its life it is 20 to 30 cm long. In the river Vistula in Poland, large 6 lb specimens have been caught. This fish moves from one place to another and is a fast-growing migratory type that undertakes journeys of up to 350 miles if there are no obstacles in the form of dams and high weirs along the way.

This fish has a liking for barley, but is also caught equally well on balls of bread paste, pieces of worms, and maggots. Float fishing is the best technique, and the bait should be allowed to float close to the bottom, about 10 cm above it. The line should not rest on the water surface, but should be airborne between the float and the rod. The selected rod is a long one, at least 3 m with a fine tip and a line of 3 lb breaking strain. One to two pieces of barley are fastened to a small hook with a fine point. During fishing, the ground-bait is scattered. The largest fishes can be caught in the deepest waters. The flesh is tasty and is eaten in some places.

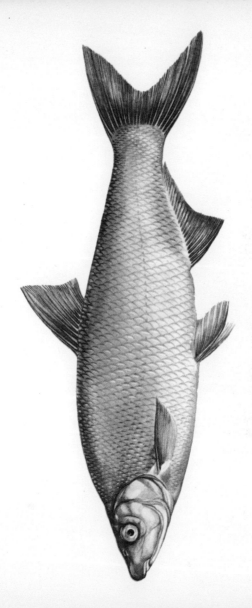

Vimba vimba

Pelecus cultratus

This fish is one of the lesser known, but is still a very interesting type of Carp family. It is similar to Bleak in its body shape and coloration. Its toothless mouth is in a high position. Its extended pectoral fins reach as far as the ventral ones. It is characterized by a zig-zag lateral line and a sharp scaleless underside. The head has striking large eyes. It grows to a weight of 1 lb and occasionally to 2 lb.

Pelecus cultratus is found in rivers and dams in the hinterland of the Baltic, Caspian and Black Seas. Although it usually lives in sea water it can travel far up the rivers. In the Danube it frequents the bays in the bends of the river, where it lives mainly on various insects. Larger individuals also eat larval fishes. It can adjust to changing living conditions, for example those following the construction of river dams.

Pelecus cultratus spawns in spring in midstream, where the female deposits several thousand eggs, which float freely with the current.

Occasionally this species can be caught when fly fishing for Asp or when it attacks a small lure. In some places it can be caught more frequently. Views on the quality of its flesh differ. It is definitely tasty when salted or smoked but it is less suitable for normal preparation.

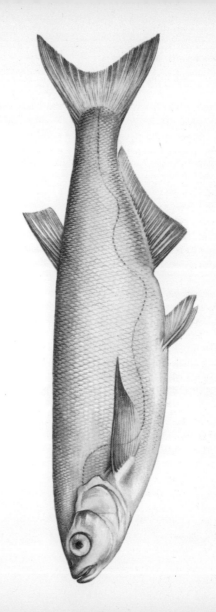

Pelecus cultratus

The Crucian Carp

Carassius carassius

This fish differs from the Carp in that it has a smaller head, no barbels, a silver iris and there is usually a dark fleck in front of the caudal fin, particularly in young fishes. In places where there is a deficiency of food it has a low body form, whereas in a good environment it is distinguished by the high, arched structure of its body.

The Crucian Carp exists nearly all over Europe and eastwards as far as the river Lena. Together with the Carp it has even been introduced into Asia and America. It breeds profusely in still, densely overgrown, muddy waters. It grows more slowly than the Carp, has smaller measurements and weighs up to 8 oz, although the larger specimens can weigh 12 oz. In the U.S.S.R., in Lake Chulom near the Volga, Crucian Carp of up to 10 lb have been caught.

Spawning occurs at the end of spring or the beginning of summer. The female gradually lays, in the course of several days, 100,000 to 300,000 eggs on various types of water vegetation. The dwarf variety grows to a length of 10 to 12 cm and begins to spawn when only 7 cm long. Crossbreds between the Carp and the Crucian Carp can be found, which in some cases can even be fertile. They grow more slowly than Carp, but more quickly than Crucian Carp. Such crossbreeding is sometimes performed deliberately to obtain a suitable strain to populate waters where other species have found it difficult to survive.

The Crucian Carp is a valuable angling fish. It is also an excellent bait when fishing for predators, expecially Pike, as it remains and even plays about in position on the hook beneath the float. It can also withstand transporting over large distances. Its flesh is relatively tasty, but sometimes it is accompanied by an unpleasant smell, derived from its muddy environment.

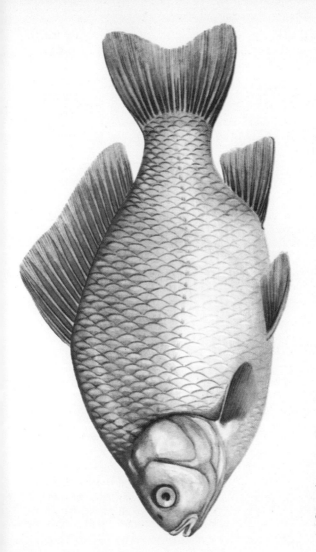

Carassius carassius

The Carp

Cyprinus carpio

Carp family
Cyprinidae

This is one of the most popular fishes in Europe, not only among anglers but also among the non-angling public. In Europe it was the first fish reared in artificial ponds, a development which soon spread extensively in some parts of Europe, such as Czechoslovakia, Poland, Germany, France and Yugoslavia. The large rivers flowing into the Mediterranean, Black, Caspian and Aral Seas were the native waters of the wild Carp which had a body that was very long, cylindrical and covered with scales. In the vicinity of the river Amur it is still found.

The Carp inhabits slow-flowing waters and moves about in shoals. It can be found in the part of the river inhabited by Bream and likes dams on the lower reaches of rivers. In winter it moves in large shoals to the slightly salty lakes adjoining the sea or even to the sea itself. At this time it grows to a length of up to 1 m and can weigh over 40 lb.

The females mature sexually in the fourth or fifth year and the males one year earlier. Carp enter shallow (20 to 40 cm deep), warm and marshy places when breeding. They spawn early in the morning. They disclose their presence in the spawning grounds by their great activity. The female sheds from many thousands to a million very small eggs, which stick to the vegetation. The fry hatch in a few days and continue to adhere to the water vegetation by their sticky glands. They first digest the contents of the yolk sack, then later start feeding on plankton before passing on to food found on the bottom, such as crustaceans and insect larvae. Owing to a natural resistance in the wild Carp to disease and adverse environmental conditions, in some places it has been put into open waters, where it hitherto did not exist.

Cyprinus carpio—wild river form

Monasteries, where fishes were regularly consumed for religious reasons, have contributed in their time to the spread of Carp from their original habitat of streams and rivers to ponds and artificial reservoirs. Current breeders have succeeded in rearing various forms; for instance a cultured Carp from such ponds has a very deep body, with an arched back and sometimes the body is only partly covered with scales, whereas at other times it is completely smooth. Even golden varieties are known. Today there is no continent with favourable climatic conditions, into which the Carp could not be imported and artificially reared. It has been introduced into America and Australia, but because it breeds prolifically it is not a very popular fish there.

Certain differences in colour also characterize the cultured Carp. Golden brown and yellow prevail over all other shades. The back is darker than the sides and the belly is yellowish white. There are even blue coloured Carp, which owe their coloration to their thin skin. Small Carp with scales can easily be mistaken for Crucian Carp, from which they only differ in respect of four barbels at the corners of their fleshy mouths. In some places the cultured Carp is anually deposited in great numbers in open waters. The product of such planted fishes is not usually very great as they are used to a protected lazy life in ponds and succumb to various diseases and the competition for food with other fishes.

The Carp has great economic value, although the demand for it is not the same everywhere. In central Europe heavy, 4 to 7 lb, Carp are popular but, for example in Java or

Cyprinus carpio—Scaly Carp

Israel, Carp which are substantially smaller, weighing only 10 to 20 oz, are sold. Carp production is rising all the time and now the fishes are intensively fed, whilst the ponds are fertilized and disinfected and the water warmed. Waters, warmed by electric power-stations, have been exploited throughout Europe with great success. For the time being they are experimental and aim at prolonging the growth period of Carp to a whole year and so substantially increasing its numbers. Almost unbelievable results have been obtained in small reservoirs with regulated conditions of temperature, oxygen and water change; the volume of fishes has become almost greater than the water volume. The fishes ate according to their appetite from automatic feeding places, and in several months they weighed 2 lb and were able to breed.

Although very temperamental and shy, the Carp is still a good sporting fish. It starts to feed at a water temperature of about 10°C. In autumn this period lasts until October or November, especially in deep water, where the water layers become cold more slowly. Fishing in autumn is regarded as the best time, as this is the period when the fish's fat reserves are at their highest for the ensuing winter. In summer, fishing can be successful early in the morning, early in the evening and at night. In autumn it is possible to anticipate catches throughout the day and certain success can be ensured by regularly feeding the fishes, although this should not be overdone as the aim is simply to keep them in one place for

Cyprinus carpio—Mirror Carp

The Carp

continued

as long as possible. They can be fed with bread paste, boiled potatoes, wheat, chaff, boiled beans, peas, sweet corn, lupin seeds and lentils. Worms can be used effectively as bait in the spring. Pieces of bread crust floating on the surface can also be effective. This method has also proved successful when fishing for Chub. Adverse conditions for fishing exist in August when algal blooms appear on the water.

All types of rod can be used, if they are long (about 3 m) and strong enough. The reel must have an effective checking mechanism. A medium strength line is selected, for example of 7 to 12 lb breaking strain. Sometimes treble hooks are used, particularly when using pieces of potato as bait, but fishing for Carp with a hook with a short shank is more sporting. When ledgering, the line should not be too slack. The Carp, when hooked, immediately moves sharply forwards.

Ledgering and float fishing from a boat is also popular. When float fishing, shallow places are most suitable or an open expanse of water near the bank. It is advisable to use sharp hooks, whilst the float should be very delicate, sensitive and correctly balanced, that is almost submerged. A good net is equally important, as this will help to land fishes on steep banks or into a boat.

Carp flesh is tasty and is pleasant when roasted, smoked, fried or marinated. Excellent soup can be made from the spawn and milt. Of all freshwater fishes it is the species with the greatest economic value.

Cyprinus carpio—Leather Carp

The Stone Loach

Noemacheilus barbatulus

Loach family

Cobitidae

This is a typical representative of the Loach family, noted for the small proportioned, elongated, cylindrical bodies of its members. The fishes of this family have a smooth body with the minute scales, set in the skin. The Stone Loach's body is yellow-brown in colour with darker blotches, thus making the fish hard to distinguish from the river bottom. It has 6 barbels at the side of its mouth. It grows to a length of about 15 cm and lives about 5 years.

The Stone Loach lives in European rivers in mountainous and semi-mountainous, gently sloping areas. However, it is not found in Norway and northern Sweden. It favours a sandy bottom where there is a possibility of hiding under various stones. If it penetrates still waters, for instance a pond, it can multiply there very quickly indeed. It travels along the bottom with jerky movements and only gives itself away by stirring up the light mud or sand. In the breeding season, from spring until July, it sheds several thousand eggs at periodic intervals. It feeds on small larvae, found on the bottom and is itself often the prey of predatory fishes.

Stone Loach used to be very popular for its delicious white flesh. It has no sporting significance, but occasionally serves as a bait fish for predators.

Noemacheilus barbatulus

The Spined Loach

Loach family

Cobitis taenia

Cobitidae

Although this fish has 6 barbels like the Stone Loach and also belongs to the Cobitidae family, it is distinguished by its characteristic two-pronged retractable spine under each eye, which is controlled by special muscles. Anglers can easily be injured by the sharp movements of this fish after it has been caught. The basic coloration of its body is a yellow-brown to orange, with 10 to 18 large dark flecks along its sides. The male can be distinguished from the female by the reinforced second ray of its pectoral fins, at the base of which there is also a special scale.

The Spined Loach is found almost everywhere in Europe, but often its presence is not known. It is absent from Scotland, Ireland, and Norway. Only modern fishing methods using electrical apparatus have shown, that this Loach is fairly numerous in streams. It lives a secluded existence and takes pleasure in places where there is fine sand, when only its head and caudal fin are to be seen sticking out from the bed. It inhabits slow-flowing and still waters, where it breeds on plant remnants or flooded vegetation. It reaches a length of 6 to 12 cm.

It has no sporting value, as its exceptionally small mouth makes it difficult to catch on a hook. Sometimes it is kept in aquaria.

Cobitis taenia

The Weatherfish
Loach family
Misgurnus fossilis   *Cobitidae*

This fish is one of the largest of the Loach family. It lives almost all over Europe, from France to the Volga in the U.S.S.R., but it is not found in Britain or Scandinavia. It has a long, yellow to brownish black, belt-like body, which is between 20 and 30 cm in length and it has 10 barbels around its mouth. Its underside is yellow to orange in colour.

It likes lower reaches of slow-flowing rivers, but can also be found in still pools. It usually lives half-hidden in the mud of side bays, swamps or completely overgrown areas. It starts looking for food with the onset of night. In waters with insufficient oxygen it makes use of an additional intestinal breathing system. With each gulp on the water surface it takes in an air bubble which travels to the back part of the intestine, where it is absorbed into the blood. At the same time it releases surplus air from the anal opening with a whistling noise. In winter it hides deep in the mud. In spring when breeding the female sheds several thousand eggs on to a tangle of water plants, usually in inaccessible places.

The Weatherfish has no economic or sporting value, but anglers regard it as good bait for catching large predatory fishes, such as Catfish. Because of its small oxygen requirements it is sometimes put into aquaria to forecast weather changes, since during sudden changes in barometric pressure it swims restlessly around the walls of the tank and periodically rises to the surface.

Misgurnus fossilis

The European Catfish

Silurus glanis

Catfish family

Siluridae

This is the heaviest and largest freshwater fish in places where the Huchen *(Hucho hucho)* is not found. A large specimen can easily be distinguished from other fishes, but a small specimen resembles in appearance the Horned Pout. Its distinctive features include 6 barbels of which the longest pair are at the corners of the upper jaw and the 4 shorter ones are on the longer lower jaw. It also has a long anal fin and a very long brown or grey-black, speckled, scaleless body. Now and then even a white Catfish can be seen, an albino variety with red eyes. In Europe the Catfish can be found in slow-flowing rivers, as far west as the Rhine and in the hinterland of the Baltic, Black, Caspian and Aral Seas. It thrives in the deep waters of dams, constructed on the lower reaches of rivers.

A wide mouth, equipped with small teeth, shows that this fish is a predator. Old Catfish mainly hunt small, insignificant types of fish and only occasionally valuable large fishes. Moreover they are not ungrateful for various larvae, shellfish, crayfish, or simply anything alive that they find on the bottom. They hunt in the evening and at night and also early in the morning. They often reveal their presence at such times by sounds reminiscent of the croaking of frogs.

Spawning occurs in late spring at a water temperature of about 19 °C, when the female prepares a nest in the shallows from roots and various plant remnants, in which she lays hundreds of thousands of large eggs. The male guards the nest for some time. The larval fishes are similar to tadpoles and tend to escape from daylight by hiding under stones. At the age of 7 years the Catfish reaches a weight of 3 to 15 lb. Older fishes put on weight more quickly than younger

Silurus glanis

ones, sometimes up to 2 to 7 lb in a year. The male can live to an age of 30 years or more. At present 60 to 100 lb fishes are often caught, sometimes even heavier ones and there are even reports of fishes weighing 550 lb and measuring 3 to 5 m.

Hunting Catfish is a highly valued sport, not only because the angler has to pit his strength against a large adversary, but also because the Catfish is a good fighter and can only be deceived by a really experienced angler. Success is most likely in the morning or early evening. At night Catfish often approach the river banks. The best time for fishing is June, especially during warm, cloudy days. It can be caught by ledgering with live or dead fishes, by surface float fishing using a large float, or even by trailing dead fishes.

Fishing with spinners, plugs and imitations of mice and frogs is regarded as the most sportsman-like method. The rod has to be 2 to 3 m long and of sufficient strength and quality. In clear parts of the river or reservoir when using artificial lures, a line of 9 to 12 lb breaking strain is adequate, but for overgrown pools and fishing with live bait on the bottom the usual strength required is 20 lb. There has always to be an adequate length of line on the reel, because when well hooked the Catfish immediately makes for the nearest hideout, in the course of which it often somersaults, hits the line with its tail and stands on its head. During the course of the contest the reel check is applied according to the strength of the fish involved. A gaff or landing net is used to land the fish. The flesh of the European Catfish is tasty and pleasant when smoked, although larger specimens can be too greasy.

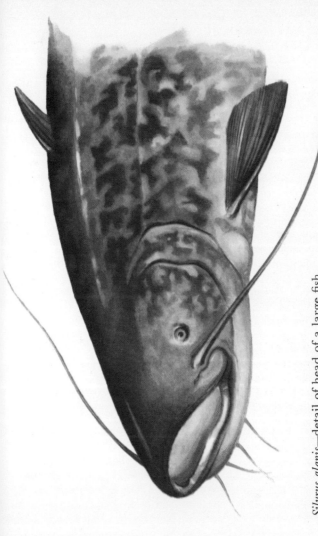

Silurus glanis—detail of head of a large fish

The Horned Pout   North-American Catfish family
Ictalurus nebulosus   *Ictaluridae*

At the end of the last century some American fishes were experimentally climatized in Europe. One of these was the Horned Pout and economic and sporting hopes were held out for this fish. It spread quickly down the Elbe, the Danube and into central Europe. It also entered the Seine, from where it penetrated other French rivers.

The Horned Pout has a naked body and 8 sensitive barbels on its head. The dorsal fin is larger than that of the Catfish and has a hard saw-edged ray. There is a small adipose fin to the rear of its back as in the Salmon family. The anal fin is considerably shorter than that of the Catfish. The body is a golden brown in colour with darker shades. It rarely reaches a weight of 1 lb, although in its homeland it can weigh over 2 lb, but does not live any longer. In European waters it usually lives up to 5 years. It breeds in June and the male looks after several thousand yellowish eggs. It looks for food on the soft bottom, especially in the evening and at night.

Anglers do not like this fish as it greedily swallows the bait with the hook deep down into its stomach before other fishes can get to it. Subsequent removal of the hook is very difficult. Anglers also complain about the sharp rays in the pectoral and dorsal fins, which have poisonous glands at their base. They can cause injuries which heal very slowly. Beginners like to fish for the Horned Pout as it is a very encouraging fish, which always rises to the bait, even though other fishes may have lost their appetites. Fishing for it in the undergrowth is usually done by float fishing or ledgering on the bottom with worms or pieces of fish. Its reddish flesh is rather greasy, but very tasty. The fish is skinned prior to preparation.

Ictalurus nebulosus

The European Eel

Anguilla anguilla

Eel family

Anguillidae

The Eel is renowned for its elongated snake-like body, which is covered with a thick skin and deep-set elliptical scales. The colour of the upper part of the body is usually dark blue to black and the belly is yellowish white. The Eel's most intriguing feature is that in order to breed it travels from the European and north African rivers to the western parts of the Atlantic Ocean, where it spawns in deep waters and then dies. The larval Eels, called leptocephali, start their long journey, which lasts up to 3 years, through the ocean back to the European coast and rivers. They may stay in fresh water for 10 to 20 years and reach a weight of 2 to 9 lb and then, as adults, they migrate back again to the sea, where they spawn and die. During their return to the sea, the yellowish colour of their belly turns to a silvery colour.

The European Eel is a nocturnal fish. It lives in hideouts during the daytime, made from twigs that have drifted ashore, or between stones in the hollows of overhanging banks and only after dusk does it set off hunting. It grows relatively slowly, according to the nutritional value of its environment. It lives on small crustaceans found on the river bed and large Eels do not refuse even large creatures, such as the crayfish. In cool rivers and lakes, for example in Ireland and Scandinavia, Eels grow even more slowly and are never as large as the fishes from waters in Denmark, Germany and Poland. As the water gradually cools during the course of the year, the Eel usually stops feeding in October and searches out deeper waters with plenty of hiding places.

Nowadays the European Eel is increasingly threatened during its river journeys by mounting water pollution and the construction of weirs and dams. Many Eels are damaged

Anguilla anguilla—from a low river course

by the turbines of power-stations. Some countries have therefore started building not only fish ladders through dams, but are also installing various electrical repellent devices to protect the fishes from the turbines. Small Eels have been transported far inland and in some places experiments have been conducted in rearing Eels in reservoirs and providing them with additional food.

Anglers identify two forms of Eel by the width of their heads. There are wide- and narrow-head varieties and the former is said to be more predatory. However, there is a whole range of intermediate stages between these two forms and it is often difficult to recognize which type is which. When fishing on an uneven bed, dead bait is used, as a live one can easily crawl away into the nearest hideout. Fishing near the bottom is preferable with a strong rod and line. Once the fish is hooked it should not be allowed to move about too much, otherwise both the catch and the hook are lost. Eels can be expected to bite not only after dark, but also during the day normally, especially during changes of weather, and before a storm. When unhooking, care must be taken to avoid injury, as the wound can easily become inflamed, for Eel's blood contains a poison, which effects the heart and the central nervous system. The effect of the poison is destroyed by heat during cooking.

Although fishing for Eels is very exciting, interest in it amongst anglers and consumers is very variable. It is popular in central Europe, but some British anglers do not care for it much.

The European Eel is a gourmet's delight, whether marinated, smoked or in oil, despite being considerably greasy.

Anguilla anguilla—from a trout river

The Burbot

Cod family

Lota lota

Gadidae

The Burbot is one of few representatives of the Cod family, which inhabit fresh waters all their lives. It has a wide, flat head with a mouth equipped with small fine teeth and one barbel on the lower jaw. There is one short and one long fin on its back. The body is smooth and slippery with very fine circular scales. The brown-black speckled body is cylindrical in shape and narrows towards the tail. Its sides are punctuated by irregular flecks in black or brown and sometimes even a clear yellow. Its underside is light.

This fish lives a secluded life in the cold waters of northern Europe, in the company of the Trout and the Alpine Bullhead. It is often labelled as a rapacious predator, which voraciously swallows everything alive. This is only true, however, of Burbot living in waters inhabited by Trout or other members of the Salmon family, when they have to compete with these for food and when they eat their fry and spawn. In contrast, in large expanses of lakes and reservoirs it lives on smaller, insignificant fishes. The contents of the digestive organs of a Burbot, living in such an area, revealed a variety of types of less valuable fishes, such as small Perch, Ruffe, Stickleback, Roach and Bream. The Burbot usually weighs about 4 lb and is 50 to 70 cm long; the most frequent weight in Trout rivers is about 1 lb. It thrives best in the colder regions of the north, where it reaches weights of up to 40 lb. It is worth noting that it is most active in the period when the activity of other freshwater fishes is decreasing, that is at low temperatures below 7°C. It breeds at the end of December and the beginning of January, when the female lays several hundred thousand eggs, though the largest fishes lay up to 5,000,000. Each of these is smaller than a pin head.

Lota lota

The Burbot

continued

In northern Europe it is a popular sport to catch Burbot in holes cut into the ice. This fish can also be caught in flowing water during warm summer days especially, and when there are variable temperatures or changes in barometric pressure, before a storm and in water disturbed by rain. On moonless nights it is advisable to make a fire, as according to Siberian hunters the flames attract this fish. As the breeding season approaches, its search for food becomes most active and therefore the best months for catching it are November and December. In the evening the line should be cast near its daytime haunts, such as a derelict weir or groups of large stones; at night it is best hunted in the shallows, where it comes after its prey. The bait must rest on the bottom or close to it. When one Burbot bites, a catch of many others can be anticipated. It can swallow live or dead bait fishes, a bunch of worms and even get a crayfish's tail deep into its gullet. It does not fight much when hooked. After swallowing the bait it stays a while in one place and then swims slowly away. If it is near the water surface, it may start leaping or somersaulting and at night reveals itself by the splashing. When fishing in the evening a phosphorescent float is used, but at night a small bell on the tip of the rod is more suitable.

The Burbot's flesh is relatively dry but very tasty. The liver is considered the best product and is much finer than Cod liver. A restorative eye medicine used to be made from the liver fat, whilst the decorative parts of saddles, coats and other articles are made from the Burbot's skin.

Lota lota—lake form, detail of head of a large fish

The Large-mouth Bass

Micropterus salmoides

Bass family

Centrarchidae

This fish was imported into Germany almost a hundred years ago, but did not fulfil the expectations of European breeders. It has also been introduced into Britain. In its homeland in central America it is a valuable sporting fish, commonly found in many lakes and rivers. The body is brown-green and its wide mouth with overlapping lower jaw shows that it is a predator. It thrives in warm reservoirs with clear water and plenty of water plants.

The Large-mouth Bass breeds in May and June, when the female lays about 10,000 eggs in a prepared spot. They are subsequently looked after by the male. It looks for its food near the bottom. The largest Bass prey on shoals of small fishes, particularly in the evening, when, in pursuit of food, they rise to the surface. During the day the fish stays in deeper waters. In its native land it sometimes weighs over 11 lb, but in Europe the average is 1 lb.

This fish provides excellent sport and its fighting spirit can be compared to that of the Salmon family. It is caught on metal lures, artificial rubber fishes, small wooden plugs, artificial worms and frogs, flies, bunches of small worms, small live fishes, trailed dead fishes or tadpoles. When hooked it resists ferociously, leaping high out of the water as it tries to get rid of the lure or other bait. It is a gregarious fish that lives in shoals and so it is sometimes possible to catch several small fishes in the same spot. The largest specimens like to take advantage of various hiding places, such as clumps of vegetation, flooded bushes and rocky places.

The flesh is very tasty and some anglers like to cook it in a frying pan when camping.

Micropterus salmoides

The Pumpkinseed
Lepomis gibbosus

Bass family
Centrarchidae

The native waters of this fish are in the north-eastern part of the U.S.A. The Pumpkinseed became widespread with the distribution of Carp fry, so that nowadays it is a numerous and unwelcome fish in many places. Its flat body is short, yet deep and speckled with dark flecks, which even reach the fins. The iris and flecks on the gill covers are red. It lives on small organisms and the spawn and fry of its own and other fishes. For a short time the male looks after its own offspring in its plate-shaped nest.

It is caught by float fishing, using a small hook on a line of 1 to 3 lb breaking strain with animal bait. A good water bailiff prevents its overbreeding.

Owing to its small size and numerous bones it is not commonly eaten, although its flesh is relatively tasty.

The Three-spined Stickleback
Gasterosteus aculeatus

Stickleback family
Gasterosteidae

The typical feature of this fish is the three spines in front of the dorsal fin. The mouth is in an elevated, superior position. It grows up to 5 to 8 cm and lives 3 years. It used to be widespread only along the northern coast of Europe, but today it can also be found in central Europe. It is a popular aquarium fish.

In the spawning season the males have dark red bellies and olive green backs. In the maze of vegetation the males build nests, in which they later guard the eggs. The female lays 60 to 400 of them. This fish has no economic or sporting significance, although it is used for making fish flour.

Lepomis gibbosus (above)
and *Gasterosteus aculeatus* (below)

The Pikeperch

Stizostedion lucioperca

Perch family

Percidae

This fish is one of the most economically important of the Perch family. In the post glacial period it penetrated the rivers of central Europe from the east and moved as far west as the river Elbe. By the end of the eighteenth century it was being successfully reared in reservoirs and ponds, particularly in Czechoslovakia. It also thrives in dams in valleys. It has a long body and its jaws with sharp teeth stretch behind the eyes. The large 'dog teeth' in the front of the mouth are a typical feature of this fish. It has transverse dark lines at the sides and its eyes have a peculiar glassy, almost opalescent, shine. When breeding the males have a dark marble pattern on the belly.

The Pikeperch is a predatory fish and regularly feeds on Ruffe, Perch and other types of fish. It hunts for food in groups and the small specimens move about in shoals. According to size the female lays 10,000 to 500,000 eggs in spring when the temperature is between 10 and 12°C. For this purpose a place on the sandy bed is prepared beforehand. The male diligently looks after the nest for several days. The pairs spawn sometimes in shallow water and at a depth of several metres at other times. In the first year of its life the Pikeperch grows on average 10 to 15 cm and by the time it is eight years old may have reached 70 cm. Increases in weight in older fishes are higher than in younger ones; the females grow more quickly than the males whilst migratory types grow more quickly than those staying in one place. The largest Pikeperch weigh 20 to 30 lb and there are reports of fish, weighing 40 lb and being over 130 cm long. During the day they stay in deep water, but in the evening and at night they swim to the river bank after food. The Pikeperch, therefore, can be caught at

Stizostedion lucioperca

night. It can live in relatively salty water, as for example off the Baltic coast.

It provides good sport and its popularity is increasing all the time. The whole of the second half of the year is suitable for fishing for it. A catch can most likely be expected shortly after spawning or in the autumn. During the warmer times of the year fishing is best in the evening, whereas in the autumn a catch can be anticipated all day, particularly during changes in the weather. It can be caught by ledgering and float fishing, using live or dead fishes. In places where there is an uneven bed, Bleak can be chosen as live bait since they continually try to get to the surface. Equally successful is the use of dead Ruffe or Perch, made buoyant by the attachment of a piece of cork. A line of 9 lb breaking strain is strong enough and to this is directly tied a single or a double hook. When fishing near the surface of a nearby river bank, the live bait is held by a steel trace as there is a danger that it might be bitten through by a Pike. When fishing on the bottom, the line is left loose and the reel left unchecked so that the fish, after it has taken the bait, is absolutely free, since if it feels the slightest resistance it will leave the bait. The fish is only usually hooked at the second bite, but if small fishes are used it can be caught sooner. When fishing with lures, small spinners are the most efficient. If it is intended to put the Pikeperch back into the water, it must be dealt with very carefully as it develops mould very easily.

The meat is excellent. It is a diet fish with a low fat content, as low as 0.2 to 0.6 per cent. The layer of fat lies outside the muscles and in the ventral cavity it grows round the internal organs, particularly the intestine. It can be prepared in many different ways.

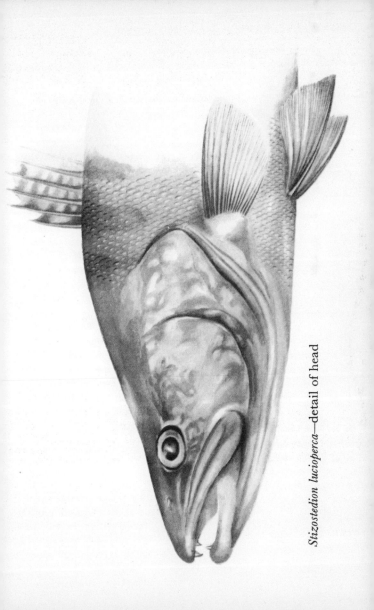

Stizostedion lucioperca—detail of head

The Eastern Pikeperch

Perch family

Stizostedion volgensis

Percidae

This fish is smaller than the Pikeperch and also has only half the number of transverse lines on its body; *Stizostedion lucioperca* has 8 to 12 lines, whereas *Stizostedion volgensis* has 5 to 7. The jaw line only stretches to the middle of the eyes. The body is stouter and has larger scales. It lives in the same type of water as the other Pikeperch, but it stays in the middle of the river in the deepest currents and the oldest part of the river bed. It can also be found in brackish water near river estuaries. It travels long journeys up river to the higher reaches, for example to the hinterland of the Black Sea.

The largest specimens are 40 cm long and reach a weight of about 2 lb usually in the third to fifth year of their life. Occasionally fishes larger than 30 cm and heavier than 14 oz are found. The large fishes prey on shoals of fry and eat small Perch and Ruffe. The smaller fishes search for crustaceans clinging to the river bed.

There is not much difference in fishing for *Stizostedion volgensis* or *Stizostedion lucioperca;* perhaps only the size of bait should vary. The uninformed angler usually has difficulty in distinguishing between these two very similar fishes. Fishing is more rewarding during the colder, autumn weather, when they are very active in their search for food. In some places this fish has an economic value, but its importance as a game fish is relatively small.

The Eastern Pikeperch's flesh is of the same taste and quality as that of the Pikeperch.

Stizostedion volgensis

The Perch
Perca fluviatilis

Perch family
Percidae

In coloration this is one of the most beautiful freshwater fishes. It frequents the reaches of river, lake or dam where Bream and Barbel are found. It can be found almost everywhere in Europe, even in places where it did not originally exist, for example in Scotland. It has a sizeable double dorsal fin, the first or larger part of which is supported by sharp spiky thorns. The ventral, anal and caudal fins are orange, edged in blood red. The back part of the arched body is a dark, blue-green. Five to nine dark stripes start here and extend to the light lower third of the body. Hard, comblike, ctenoid scales give the body a rough surface. This roughness is caused by small spikes on the outer edge of the scales. The opercular bones are equipped with a sharp thorn, which has to be watched when the hook is being released from the Perch's mouth.

Perch stay in shoal near the bottom and around bushes or groups of stones. They chase their prey in shoals too. The largest shoals are formed by small Perch, as the larger ones move about in smaller groups. They breed in April or May near the river banks where the female lays long bands of 15,000 to 20,000 eggs. Cannibalism is quite common among them and one-year-old Perch often eat their own fry. Until they are 15 cm long they live on invertebrate organisms. Then they start their predatory existence. The rate of growth is determined by their numbers and the food available in the reservoir or river. Fifteen year old Perch can weigh 3 lb, but cases of both slower and faster growth are known, for example in the U.S.S.R. and Finland they can weigh up to 9 lb. Sometimes they multiply too much and compete for food with other species of fish. Near the shore in large expanses of water, slow-growing Perch are found

Perca fluviatilis

and in open water they grow much more quickly. Fish economists wage a protracted war with this fish. In Ireland, Sweden and Scotland there are Trout lakes, where the population of Perch had to be removed to restore the original character of such lakes.

Large sized Perch are a favourite, much sought after fish. It is possible to fish for them by rod all year round. A light, springy rod with a reel and fine line is used and the float and weight are quite small. The bait should be about 15 cm above the bottom; in this connection slow-moving maggots have proved to be effective and in summer grasshoppers, but small bait fishes are best at the end of the year. The bait need not cover the whole hook, but it must be moving. The catch is sometimes accompanied to the surface by another two or three Perch.

For normal purposes a spinner is the artificial lure selected. The Perch likes a red colour, but can be attracted equally well by golden and black speckled or striped lures and by those with red beads or a fringe. During fishing the angler must move about from place to place and actively search for the Perch.

Fishing for Perch under the ice is widespread in northern countries. Winter fishermen are equipped with chisels, drills and perforated scoops to remove the drift ice. Short rods with a bait in the form of a one-hook lure are used. They are raised and let down into the hole. Several holes in various places are prepared and the haul from such fishing is substantial. The Perch's flesh has few bones, is quite dry and when roasted and rubbed over with garlic is a delicacy even for gourmets.

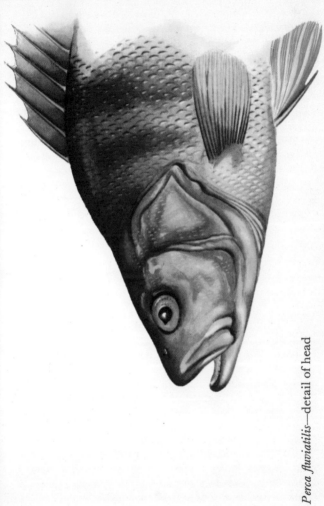

Perca fluviatilis—detail of head

Zingel zingel

Zingel zingel inhabits the river Danube and some of its larger tributaries. Its head is well flattened and the body shape is similar to the Pikeperch's. It is long with a very narrow tail base. Dark flecks and 4 to 5 transverse stripes in the form of wide dark lines are scattered over its yellowish brown body. The anal and rear dorsal fins are located almost exactly in line with one another although the anal fin is a little shorter. It usually grows to a length of 40 cm and a weight of 10 oz. It breeds in spring on the gravelly bottom in mid-stream. It stays in deep water and only now and then is there a chance of catching it. It lives on food of the river bed, but given the chance will eat larval fishes.

Zingel streber

This fish looks very much like *Z. zingel* but it is smaller and is characterized by its slender tapering body. It also lives in the river Danube and some of its tributaries. It is active after dark and mainly during the night when it looks for food. Fishing for it is most often successful at this time and it is usually caught when fishing for other fishes. By and large it remains on the bottom, in the relatively strong and deep currents, where it also breeds.

Both these species have an underdeveloped air-bladder and progress along the bottom in characteristic darting movements. They have no economic or sporting value. The taste of their flesh is of average quality.

Zingel zingel

Zingel streber

The Ruffe (Pope)

Gymnocephalus cernua

Perch family

Percidae

The Ruffe is the smallest member of the Perch family (Percidae). Its body is slimy and brown-green in colour, with a number of flecks in longitudinal stripes. The first or longer part of the flecked dorsal fin is equipped with sharp rays. Sharp spikes can also be found jutting from the opercular bones on the head. Injuries to anglers caused by these thorns are frequent and unpleasant.

The Ruffe lives in still or slow-flowing waters and can be found almost everywhere in northern and central Europe, except for Ireland and Scotland. It likes deep water with deposits of sand and gravel. It spawns in spring, later than the Perch, and can breed quickly wherever it is located. It competes for food with fishes feeding on bottom-living organisms, for example Carp, Bream and Eel. To achieve a similar rate of growth to the Bream, it has to eat seven times more food. It grows very slowly and barely survives 6 years. It reaches a length of 10 to 15 cm, although in large Russian rivers and off the coast of the Bay of Finland it can reach a length of 30 cm.

It is active after dusk, when it leaves the deeps and comes inshore. It swims about in shoals and other Ruffe are not discouraged when one is caught. In winter it hides in deep hollows, but can be caught through holes in the ice. When fishing for the Ruffe, larger hooks with a longer shank are used and small bait, such as wriggling maggots attached by their tips. The Ruffe is quickly attracted by live bait and swallows it greedily complete with hook. It is mainly used as a bait fish for catching Pikeperch. Although it is a small fish, its flesh is tasty and soup made from it is excellent.

Gymnocephalus cernua

Gymnocephalus schraetzer

Perch family
Percidae

Gymnocephalus schraetzer, a close relative of the Ruffe, lives in the watershed of the river Danube, but mainly in the river itself. As opposed to the former species, this fish has a more slender, elongated body with a more pointed head. The sides of the body are yellowish with 2 to 3 longitudinal stripes, which easily identify it. It likes to stay in deep currents on the gravelly river bed.

This fish does not reach large proportions and grows to a length of 20 cm and a weight of 2 oz. Breeding takes place in spring on the gravel, where the female sheds several thousand small eggs. Various insect larvae and bottom-living organisms form the main food supply. When other fishes are breeding, their spawn and fry are eaten in addition.

G. schraetzer is not fished anywhere in large numbers and so has no economic importance. It is only an occasional catch. Fishing techniques are the same as those employed for Ruffe, and again like the Ruffe it makes good bait for catching Pikeperch.

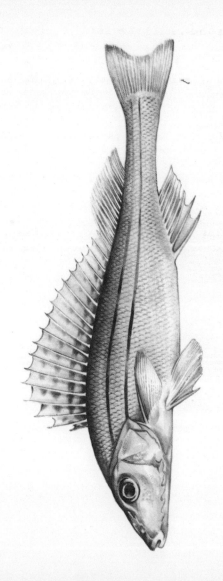

Gymnocephalus schraetzer

The Alpine Bullhead
Cottus poecilopus

Bullhead family
Cottidae

This fish differs from the former species by the even greater width of its large mouth, by a greater flattening of the head but mainly in the regular stripes of its ventral fins. It inhabits rivers adjacent to the Baltic Sea, the watershed of the river Danube and the rivers to the east as far as the Amur. Its other biological features are very similar to the former species and in some places they live together. It is also a popular bait for Trout and is often found hidden under stones.

The Miller's Thumb
Cottus gobio

Bullhead family
Cottidae

The representatives of the Bullhead family (Cottidae) largely inhabit the coastal waters of seas and oceans. Their body is spindle-shaped and narrowing towards the tail.

The Miller's Thumb is a freshwater species with a very wide mouth and fine teeth. It has a bony armour on the sides of its head and a sharp thorn on its gill covers. It adapts its coloration to its environment. It can be found in the Trout waters of central and eastern Europe, which are clear, cold and well oxygenated. During the day it usually hides under flat stones. It moves with jerky leaps. In spring it sticks several hundred large yellow-orange eggs on to the underside of stones away from the main water currents. According to the latest data, neither Miller's Thumb nor Alpine Bullhead compete with Trout for food and they themselves occasionally provide an incidental part of the diet of large Trout. It is usually 10 cm long and lives for 3 to 5 years. It is excellent dead bait when ledgering for large Trout. Finally it is often the subject of artificial lures.

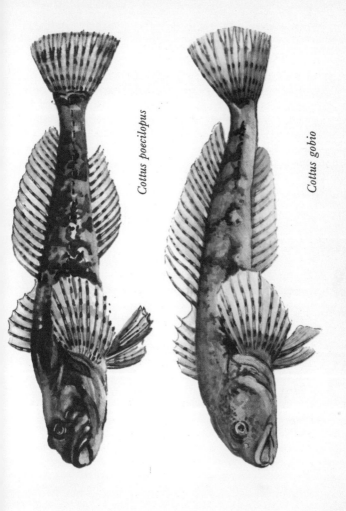

Cottus poecilopus

Cottus gobio

Fish Food

In the following two plates, typical representatives of the live organisms which form a part of the fish's staple diet are listed.

The food of all types of larval fishes or young fishes which filter their food with the help of their gills includes some types of planktonic crustaceans, such as *Daphnia* (1) and *Cyclops* (2). They live mainly in slow-flowing waters and reach a size of only several millimetres.

The muddy beds of rivers are host to red *Tubifex* (3) with segmented bodies. They live in large colonies and in places almost form a red carpet. They can also be found in badly polluted waters. Larger fishes, such as Carp, Tench and Barbel, eat small freshwater molluscs, notably pond-snails (4), which grow to a size of several centimetres. The fishes select small pond-snails, the shells of which they can crush with their pharyngeal teeth or with their muscular stomachs. Anglers do not like to see a large number of pond-snails in the water, as they eat their bait on the bottom.

Water lice (5) often provide part of the fish's diet and can be found in large numbers in still, muddy waters.

Freshwater Shrimps (6), which are a favourite food of members of the Salmon family, can be found in clear fast-flowing waters.

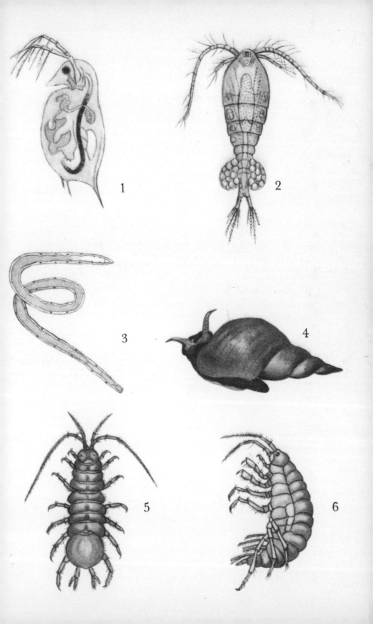

Fish Food

continued

Stonefly larvae can be found in mountain streams as they are dependent on water throughout their complicated life cycle. Their larvae (1) cling to the underside of stones or plant growth and are less mobile than Mayfly larvae. After sloughing several times, they crawl up the river bank and change into adult insects (2). They lay their eggs straight on to the water surface or just under it.

Mayflies are insects with a similar life pattern. Apart from mountain streams, they sometimes frequent lowland waters. They have three bristles at the end of the abdomen. Their larvae (3) are predatory and hide under the stones near the bottom. After a while the larvae change into water nymphs, which can breathe the air on the surface. They shed their skin several times during growth and at the end change into mature winged insects (4). Stoneflies and Mayflies are the originators of many types of artificial flies. Red midge larvae (5) are often a part of the fish's food and mainly stay on the river bed. They too go through the change to adult insects in the water. Fishes, particularly Carp, Bream, and Ruffe, search for them in still, muddy waters.

Anglers like to fish using Caddis Fly larvae. Adult Caddis Flies (6) look very much like small butterflies. Their larvae (7) construct various protective shells or tubes, made up of small stones and small pieces of wood, and with these they move about from one place to another.

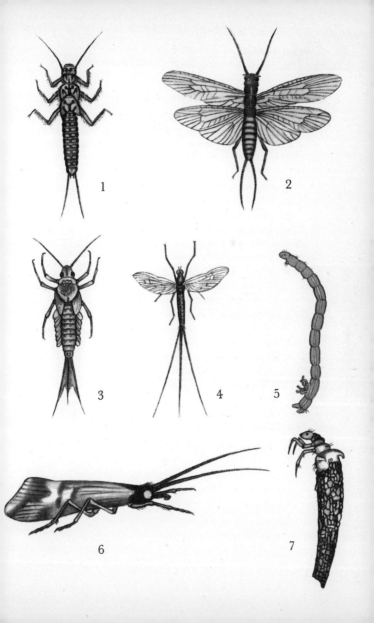

Flies

The development of fly fishing started at the beginning of the twentieth century. The pattern of this development of artificial flies has always been controlled by British anglers. The development of the industry is closely connected with the increasing interest in fishing for members of the Salmon family, such as Trout, Salmon, Charr, and only recently with fishing for members of other families, such as the Carp and Perch.

Anglers usually divide artificial flies into two basic groups. The first being wet flies, the second dry flies. These groups contain imitations of various winged insects, which are borne along by the water surface. Wet flies, as opposed to dry ones, can be used at any depth and can therefore also be weighted down. They are made from soft ungreased feather, which absorbs water easily. As a result of being continually soaked through, their shape is constantly changing. In contrast dry flies do not alter shape and always stay on the surface. They are therefore attached to smaller, lighter hooks and can be greased with a special fly fishing oil. In fast currents only one dry fly at a time is used, but on a calm surface two can be used. Wet flies are often used in threes.

The wealth of different species in the insect kingdom has produced a wide range of flies, which are available on the market. Some of them are illustrated on the opposite plate. An angler can usually manage with several of the basic types in different sizes.

Artificial Baits

Artificial baits are imitations of various aquatic animals. Many of these have fantastic, original shapes and are therefore sometimes called phantoms. The fishes bite them willingly from under or on the water surface. Although artificial baits vary in shape and colour, they are unexpectedly successful. They are particularly popular for catching Salmon, Sea Trout and some other fishes not only in fresh but also in sea water.

Imitations of the nymphal form of various insects are most commonly on sale. Also available are the range of large fantastic flies often combined with spinning vanes. They fulfil the role of metal lures and flies at the same time and attract not only Trout, but also Perch or Pike. Imitations of various fishes made from plastics (such as the Lamprey) can be used with success for all predators. Excellent baits for catching Large-mouth Bass, Perch and Pike are artificial worms, mice and frogs.

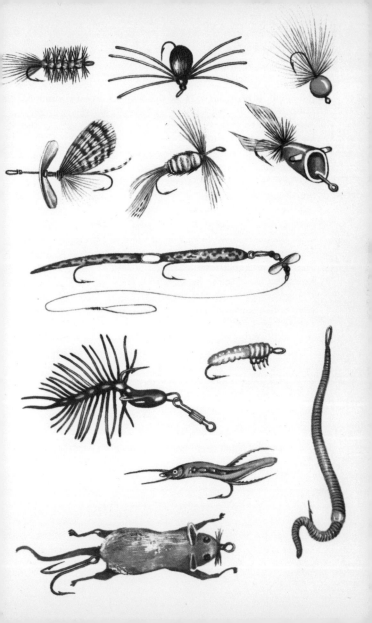

Artificial Lures

Artificial lures are some of the best known artificial baits for catching fishes. When retrieved from the water they make irregular, twisting and sometimes rotating movements, which are increased by stopping reeling in of the line and by swinging the tip of the rod to make the lure imitate a fish in distress. They are largely made from silver or golden coloured metals with coloured or metal-plated attachments. They vary a good deal in shape, but the most common are spoon-shaped, oval, or pear-shaped. Their surface can be perforated in a variety of ways; it can be incised or impressed with the pattern of scales and the names of manufacturers. They are often combined with coloured beads or coloured fringes. Treble hooks are firmly attached to the body of the lure or to the rotating parts.

Lightweight lures are useful in calm water and heavy ones in fast currents. The size of the lure is also related to its task. Lures up to 5 cm long will be sufficient for Trout, but for catching Catfish, Pike and Huchen lures larger than 8 to 12 cm are selected. Sometimes a small predator will attack large lures out of all proportion to its size and *vice versa*; it depends on the angle from which the fish sees them in the water.

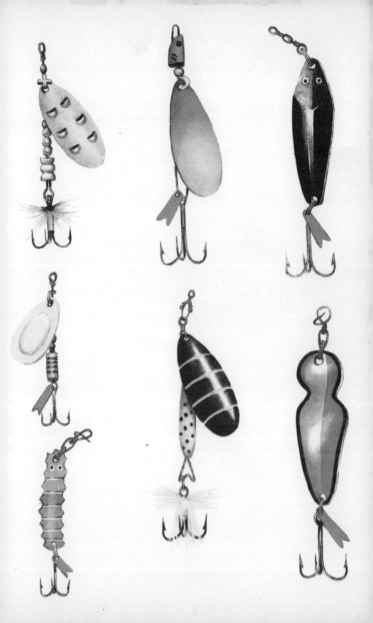

Artificial Lures

continued

Heinz lures in the shape of a fish's body can at present be regarded as common ones and are generally well known to anglers. They usually have a treble hook in the tail section or sometimes behind the head. They are clear silver or golden in colour and sometimes both. Lures in the shape of a spoon or kidney are silver or golden in colour or a combination of both. Those with a metal-plated surface, with scale impressions, or a red eye are also effective.

Oval, metal imitations of the fish's body are equally popular, such as golden or silver Devon Minnows used for catching Trout and Grayling. On the body of these is a pair of vanes which cause it to revolve around a central wire mount. They may be in various colours, not only golden and silver, and are also made from non-metallic materials. They are most often equipped with a single treble hook. Lures may have various shapes and come in a countless number of different sizes.

There are a profusion of types on the market and a separate book would have to be devoted to them to do them justice.

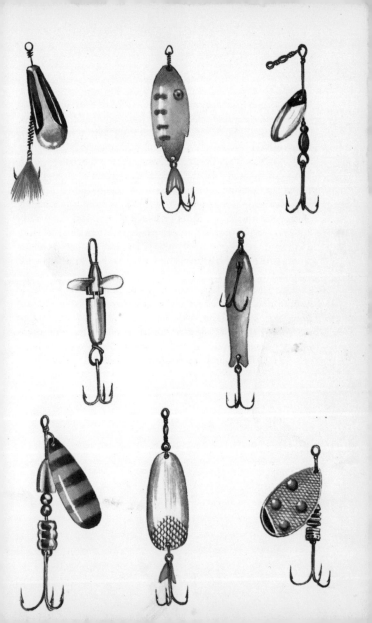

Plugs

Plugs or wooden imitations of various fishes were introduced into Europe from the U.S.A. during the second half of the last century. They are regarded as excellent artificial baits which give good results when fishing for various predatory fishes, such as Pike, Perch, Salmon, Pikeperch or Chub.

Various colours can be profitably applied to such plugs, which are produced in various sizes and weights, ranging from 0.08 to 1 oz. Red and white combinations are most often recommended, although black stripes and variegated dots in combination with various materials can be commonly seen. Quite often pieces of coloured leather, feathers or pieces of metal are suspended from the main body into which glass eyes can be set.

Light coloured plugs are useful in muddy waters, while darker shapes are useful in crystal clear rivers. There are plugs for sale which float on the water surface. When employing these, the line is reeled in slowly and the occasional sharp jerk of the rod tip makes them dip partly or completely for a moment beneath the surface.

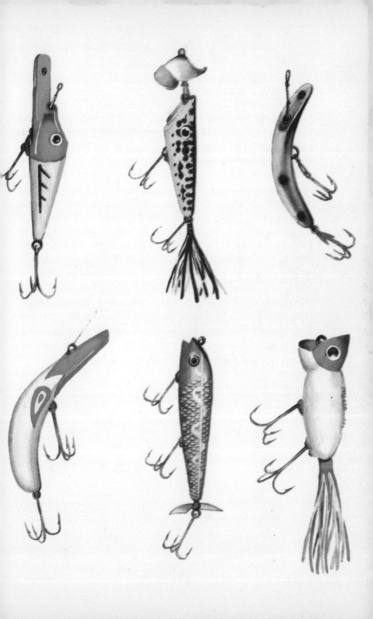

Plugs
continued

Semi-submerged plugs are another type, which when retrieved, sink to a depth of 2 m at the most, according to the speed at which the line is being recoiled. Their upper surface is usually at an angle, while pieces of metal and body incisions are added to promote a wavy motion.

Submerged plugs are those which, after being cast into the water, start sinking to the bottom. The depth at which they are trailed is selected according to requirements. Plugs with a heavy, metal lip at the front end of the body, which makes them sink, are used for ledgering behind a boat.

A number of intermediate types of plug, with various additional devices, exist also. Types with an incised head, called darters, are quite common. The addition of vanes or propellers often helps to produce sound effects to imitate the distress signals emitted by a fish when chased by a predator. In other cases treble hooks are positioned on the body in different places. Slender plugs, called Rapalas, in the shape of a fish with two treble hooks and metal strips for ventral fins are equally popular.

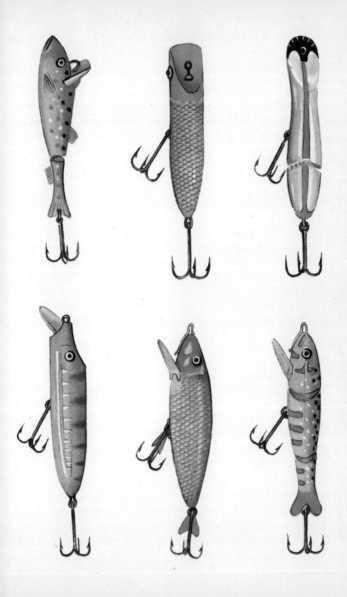

Reels

The reel was first used in China as long ago as 2,000 years, but only in this century has it become an indispensable item of the angler's equipment. At present no anglers manage with only one type or one size. The largest sizes are used in vast stretches of water when fishing for large fishes, which can run out hundreds of metres of line from a rod. Smaller reels are selected when fishing for smaller fishes in confined spaces.

Some of the more common types of reels in use are illustrated in the colour plates. Fly fishing reels (1, 3, 4) are among the simplest types, both mechanically and in terms of shape, they were gradually developed from ordinary reels (2). They act as a store for the fly fishing line and differ in size and standards. Generally the largest fly fishing reels are used when fishing for Salmon, Sea Trout or other large fishes caught by flies. A smaller, centre-pin reel is sufficient to catch Brown Trout and Grayling. On their outer edge there are often holes, which prevent such reels from becoming too heavy and help the recoiled line to dry out easily. The line is led from the reel through an eye made of some hard, smooth material, such as agate. All modern fly fishing reels have some type of checking equipment based on different principles. The most modern even have automatic recovery devices built into them. Reels can be in a normal (1,4) or horizontal (3) position. Fully automatic reels (3) have drums of various sizes, depending on the thickness of the line and the nature of the checking mechanism (3a).

Reels

continued

The first fixed-spool reels only started being produced in about 1905. The reel is attached to the rod in such a way that its axis during casting coincides with the axis of the rod, so that the coils of the line can be easily released. The spool has been extensively modified. These first fixed-spool reels (5, 6) had already a permanently positioned spool and the line was recoiled evenly. They are now produced in various sizes and their spools take a varying length of line. The recoiling process is always regulated by a system of gears and the great majority of fixed-spool reels have what is termed a 'slipping clutch' built into their mechanism. This helps to tire out and beat the heaviest fish. Improved versions have a central line position (6) and changeable metal or plastic spools, from which the line is drawn by the weight of the bait.

The multiplier reel (7), with its very fine revolving and geared spool, is used for casting heavy baits. At present they are widespread in the U.S.A. and northern Europe, where a well-known Swedish make is the *Ambassadeur* made by *ABU*. All modern types have an automatic line control (5a). The largest multipliers are used for fishing in sea water.

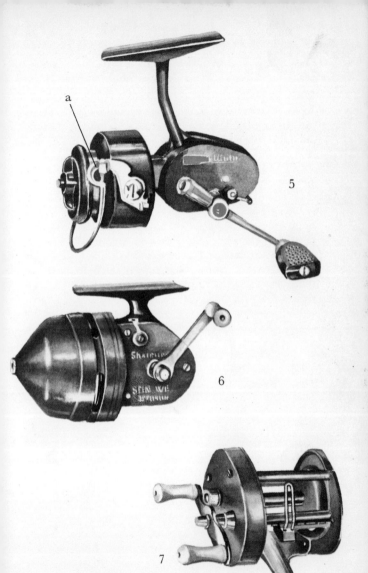

a

5

6

7

INDEX OF COMMON NAMES

Alpine Bullhead	226	Freshwater Houting	118
Alpine Charr	108		
Asp	148—150	Grayling	122
		Gudgeon	156
Barbel	164		
Bass, Large-mouth	206	Horned Pout	196
Bitterling	160	Houting	120
Bleak	162	Houting, Freshwater	118
Bream	168	Huchen	114
Bream, Silver	166		
Brook Trout	110—112	Lake Trout	98
Brown Trout	88—96	Large-mouth Bass	206
Bullhead, Alpine	226	Loach, Spined	188
Burbot	202—204	Loach, Stone	186
Carp	178—184	Miller's Thumb	226
Carp, Crucian	176	Minnow	144
Catfish, European	192—194		
Charr	106	Nase	158
Charr, Alpine	108		
Chub	134—136	Orfe	140
Common Sturgeon	74		
Crucian Carp	176	Perch	216—218
		Pike	124—128
Dace	138	Pikeperch	210—212
		Pikeperch, Eastern	214
Eastern Pikeperch	214	Pope	222
Eel, European	198—200	Pout, Horned	196
European Catfish	192—194	Pumpkinseed	208
European Eel	198—200		

Rainbow Trout	100—104	Sturgeon, Common		74
Roach	130—132			
Rudd	146	Tench		152—154
Ruffe	222	Three-spined		
		Stickleback		208
Salmon	76—80	Trout, Brook		110—112
Sea Trout	82—86	Trout, Brown		88—96
Silver Bream	166	Trout, Lake		98
Spined Loach	188	Trout,		
Sterlet	72	Rainbow		100—104
Stickleback,		Trout, Sea		82—86
Three spined	208			
Stone Loach	186	Weatherfish		190

INDEX OF LATIN NAMES

Abramis ballerus	170	Ictalurus nebulosus	196
Abramis brama	168		
Acipenser ruthenus	72	Lepomis gibbosus	208
Acipenser sturio	74	Leuciscus cephalus	134—136
Alburnoides bipunctatus	142	Leuciscus idus	140
Alburnus alburnus	162	Leuciscus leuciscus	138
Anguilla anguilla	198—200	Lota lota	202—204
Aspius aspius	148—150		
		Micropterus salmoides	206
Barbus barbus	164	Misgurnus fossilis	190
Blicca bjoerkna	166		
		Noemacheilus barbatulus	186
Carassius carassius	176		
Chondrostoma nasus	158	Pelecus cultratus	174
Cobitis taenia	188	Perca fluviatilis	216—218
Coregonus albula	116	Phoxinus phoxinus	144
Coregonus lavaretus	118		
Coregonus oxyrhynchus	120	Rhodeus sericeus amarus	160
Cottus gobio	226	Rutilus rutilus	130—132
Cottus poecilopus	226		
Cyprinus carpio	178—184	Salmo gairdneri	100—104
		Salmo salar	76—80
Esox lucius	124—128	Salmo trutta fario	88—96
		Salmo trutta lacustris	98
Gasterosteus aculeatus	208	Salmo trutta trutta	82—86
Gobio gobio	156	Salvelinus alpinus	106
Gymnocephalus cernua	222	Salvelinus fontinalis	110—112
Gymnocephalus schraetzer	224	Salvelinus salvelinus	108
		Scardinius erythrophthalmus	146
Hucho hucho	114	Silurus glanis	192—194

Stizostedion lucioperca 210—212
Stizostedion volgensis   214

Thymallus thymallus   122
Tinca tinca   152—154

Vimba vimba   172

Zingel streber   220
Zingel zingel   220